Clearly Creative CVs

Write a winning CV for the Television, Animation and other Creative Industries

Gavin Ricketts

Design by Lewis Darby, Napoleon Creative, www.napoleoncreative.com

Matador
9 Priory Business Park,
Wistow Road, Kibworth Beauchamp,
Leicestershire. LE8 0RX
Tel: (+44) 116 279 2299
Fax: (+44) 116 279 2277
Email: books@troubador.co.uk
Web: www.troubador.co.uk/matador

ISBN 978 1780883 472

British Library Cataloguing in Publication Data.
A catalogue record for this book is available from the British Library.

Typeset by Troubador Publishing Ltd, Leicester, UK

Matador is an imprint of Troubador Publishing Ltd

Printed and bound in the UK by TJ International, Padstow, Cornwall

For the S.K. who taught me how not to be a producer
and the S.K. who taught me how to be one.

Praise for the Clearly Creative Experience

Clearly Creative CVs is based on the cv4.tv workshops Gavin Ricketts developed to help film and television crew write more effective CVs. Here are testimonials from some of those who have attended.

I found Gavin's workshop an invaluable wake-up call: if your CV isn't up to scratch then you won't get that job, even if you deserve it! His comments were to the point, practical and motivating. I was able to come up with a new version that hit the spot almost straightaway.

Caroline

Gavin has such a great teaching method, and made learning so easy. I would thoroughly recommend the workshop!

Mel

Gavin helped me get some valuable perspective on my achievements and highlight my skills in a concise, direct way. His insights have really helped me focus on my strengths and given me more confidence to approach potential employers.

Rachel

Preoccupied with looking for jobs, I'd neglected the key ingredient: my CV. Gavin has a real talent in finding areas for improvement, and instantly helped me see the shortcomings in my CV.

Phil

Gavin delivers the goods directly and clearly, making sure that each individual's CV is addressed and analysed in such a way that you are learning more than expected. The session was friendly and inspiring.

Rani

It's really helped me to bring out my strengths and experience and present it on the page for someone to easily take in and comprehend. I was surprised by all my experience!

Jody

Contents

Foreword

The television industry is an extremely competitive marketplace, and with the explosion in digital broadcast channels and the Internet, together with the ever increasing flow of media graduates into the workforce, learning how to stand out from the crowd has never been more important.

I have given career advice to numerous freelancers over the years, and what has been abundantly clear to me is that you can always improve on how you present yourself to a potential employer, no matter how many years you have been in the industry.

It still amazes me that talented people with all the right skills and experience can still mess up on getting that next production role simply because they have not put themselves in the best possible light.

Learning how to market yourself is essential; from your covering letter and CV to your mobile message and Twitter account, there are key techniques that should be learned and lots that must be avoided!

And what about taking the next step up in your career? Are you in a rut, stuck in second gear? Without sounding like a HR officer in a corporate bank, you should know what you want to do in 5 years' time or at least have a good idea. Yet, there are many out there who seem to take each role as it comes hoping that the next job will be the biggie they always wanted. I would say, plan it to happen that way – don't leave to it chance!

The great thing about this book is it clearly sets out how to market yourself in all stages of your career; from the budding wet-behind-ears grad, to the seasoned series producer, there is plenty in here to grapple with, no matter what rung of the ladder you're on.

Television is an exciting and very rewarding industry to work in – you will meet fantastic and talented people along the way, but the very individuals you stand back and admire didn't just arrive on the scene overnight, many would have had a focused career plan, diligently harnessing their people skills and selling themselves as *the* person a production could not do without.

A crowded market it may be but opportunities will always present themselves and it has never been a more exciting time being a freelancer in a truly multi-media landscape. So, if you want to make the most of your talent and learn how to navigate your way to a successful and fulfilling career, this book will certainly help you accomplish it.

Joe Mahoney
Managing Director, ProductionBase

Introduction

How tough is it to whittle down fifty applications for a single day's freelance work to five people to interview? If the average CV is two pages, then that's 100 pages. Surely that will take ages to sift through?

Actually, it's surprisingly easy, because a chunk of them will be discarded at first glance.

I've worked in the media for nearly two decades, on feature films, television programmes, websites and print projects, in roles from runner to creative director. I've been responsible for employing people for over ten years: researchers, camera crew, website designers and animators.

I've read thousands of curriculum vitae or CVs as they are usually known (resumé in the States) and I've learned that many share the same problems of poor design and layout, not enough of the important details, too much non-essential information, and at the end of the day, they do not actually communicate the applicant's skills with clarity.

Whenever we post a job advert at Napoleon Creative, my production company and animation studio, we get inundated with responses. We can't spend long reading each one when beginning the initial cull, so those CVs that do not hit the nail on the head hit the recycle bin pretty quickly. What I've also learned, however, is that a poor CV is not necessarily indicative of a poor applicant; their CV may not be doing justice to the senders' skills and experience. This means they're not cutting through the clutter of other applications to get them through to the interview stage.

In 2007, as a frustrated employer wading through countless poor CVs, I started to run workshops to teach creative people like you how to write a great CV for the television, film, animation and other creative industries. The ideas in the workshop are based on my 15 years of experience as a producer and writer, working within broadcast organisations, corporate communications companies and now in my own business. They've been road-tested by working crew members, who've seen a dramatic increase in the interest their applications generate because they've applied my principles to their CV and covering letter.

I've now taken the principles from the workshop and illustrated them with real-world examples in this book, so you can learn the skills you need to write an effective CV that will confidently make your skills crystal clear to any employer even at a quick scan, and get your name on the 'must interview' list.

Getting the Most out of this Book

If you've opened this book because you've just seen a great job advertised that you want to apply for and you need to update your CV as quickly as possible, I suggest you skip straight to – wait, before you do, let me tell you about my focus system.

The Focus System

As you read through the book you'll see an iris logo around some headings. I've done this to highlight to you the relative importance of each section.

No logo means this will make a difference, but you want to concentrate on the sections with logos first if you're in a hurry.

This symbol means yes, really, take this bit seriously.

This symbol means pay close attention, ignore this section at your peril, implement the tips now.

Okay, so if you're in a hurry, skip to Part 2, where the actual writing bit starts, but be sure to come back and read Part 1 when you've finished, okay?

Two Days' Hard Work

Your CV is probably the most significant document you'll ever write, since those two pages of A4 will decide the jobs you win, affecting your earning power, determining your circle of contacts and influencing the path your career takes.

You need to treat your CV with the greatest of respect, to nurture it and tend it as your career grows. If you keep it well fed and watered, it will in return keep food on your table and fill your days with interesting, challenging, fulfilling work.

If you're serious about updating your CV, or even starting one from scratch, it's not something that you'll achieve in an hour or two. If you're following the Clearly Creative process, you need to start by reading right the way through Part 1: Selling Yourself, to grasp the concept of how to sell your services. Then you can begin the writing process, which is what Part 2: Creating a Clearly Creative CV is all about.

Ideally, you'll start one Saturday morning, or first thing on a free day between jobs. Get up as though it's a work day, sit at a desk, set aside your mobile phone and get grafting. Plough through to Chapter 8 - Personal Introduction. This will probably take you till lunch. Get some food, go out and get some fresh air.

After you're back from lunch, spend the rest of the afternoon on Chapters 9 – Credits to Chapter 11 – Creative Work. It really will take you that amount of time to write up your credits, getting them structured, written and reviewed.

The next day you have available, start at 9am again and work through Chapter 12 – Training, Software and Education to Chapter 14 – References, which shouldn't take too long. From say, 11.30am till lunch, you can proof read everything you've written so far.

Coming back from lunch, start with the Chapter 15 – Branding Your CV. Moving through the book, you should complete the version control section around 4pm. Take half an hour out to watch some daytime TV, then another hour of proofing. When you're done for the day, send it out to three friends to read through. Remember to offer to proof their CV in return.

By working your way through this book on this schedule, you can have a great, clearly creative CV in two day's work.

Calculating the Benefit

So what will this cost you? This book is priced at £12.99. Add to that the two day's work I've described above. Maybe you charge £250 a day, that's £500 you've not earned. Suddenly, that's £513 you're out of pocket. Wait, I'm making this sound like a really bad deal.

You have to think of the bigger picture. After employing the Clearly Creative process, crew members have seen an increase in interest in their CV and the rates they've been offered.

Let's say that for every ten jobs, you currently get an average of two interviews. Now, imagine sending out your sparkling new CV and you start getting an average of four interviews. You only need to convert one of those interviews to an extra job lasting a week to pay back over double the £513 you've invested. On the way, you've got another clip on your showreel and more contacts from which to win work.

Multiply this increase in earning and opportunities over a year, or even five years, and the Clearly Creative process could make an incredible difference to your career path.

Winning Work

You'll notice as you read through this book that I talk about 'winning work'. I like using this phrase because it sets you in the right frame of mind. Finding work is a blood sport, a tough competition. Like an athlete at the starting blocks, you need to have prepared and trained, and be on top form to win. Winning is also about celebrating victory, of being the best candidate.

Winning is also a playful word, reminding you that this is a game, and should be fun. You need to tap in to the excitement and anticipation in every application, followed with a determination to win next time if you come second or third place.

The Clearly Creative Promise

I'm not promising you that by buying this book and following its principles that you will gain untold wealth and limitless career opportunities. The Clearly Creative process is not a foolproof template that turns your CV into a golden ticket to every job which you've ever dreamed of. What I want to help you create is a mindset to be able to write a frank, accurate and compelling CV that shows all your skills in a clear way. I want you to view the way you win work with a marketing mindset so you're fully armed to take on every job application. This will hopefully lead to more interviews, so you get to meet your new employers face-to-face and win the work.

Our Survey Says

When I started my workshops, they were based on my experience alone. Some of the attendants were producers or production managers who were involved with the recruitment of crew for the productions they worked on, and my Clearly Creative process rang true with them. I wanted to see how my ideas resonated with other recruiters, so we surveyed employers from a variety of production companies, from big broadcast players to small independent producers to find out what makes them select a particular CV over others.

They gave their answers anonymously, enabling them to be free and frank with why and how they make their selection. We analysed the responses, and you'll find them referenced throughout this book as they give an incredible insight into how your CV is reviewed by employers. I also demonstrate how you can use this insight to create a more effective application.

PART 1: Selling yourself

Chapter 1

The First Moment of Truth

Marketeers talk about the First Moment of Truth. This is the name Proctor and Gamble, a leading consumer product company, gave to the moment when a consumer is in the store faced with shelves laden with choices. It's the moment when that person makes a snap decision on which product to pick up and take to the counter; a snap decision that is actually based on years of product experience, exposure to advertising and advice from friends, family, magazines, experts, celebrities and increasingly the general public through online reviews.

In your career, your First Moment of Truth is when a producer or production manager opens your cover letter and CV and begins to read. They, too, will have experience of buying similar 'products', that is they will have contracted other camera crews, web designers and make-up artists to work for them on previous projects.

They have been 'exposed to advertising', and by that I mean they have watched TV programmes, read reviews of them in newspapers and stories about the companies that made them in the industry press. When they read your CV they will have some knowledge of the broadcasters, programmes or campaigns you've worked on. They also might have anecdotal advice from colleagues or friends who have recommended your work. They might know people who've worked on the projects that you've worked on. All of these factors will influence their first experience of you, so this First Moment of Truth needs to count.

Your CV needs to communicate the skills and experience you have. The broadcasters for whom you have made programmes. The ad campaigns you've art directed. The kinds of contributors and celebrities you've worked with. The challenges of the website you've built. Which producers or production managers are willing to vouch for your performance. The kit and software you know how to use. You need to show them that you're the perfect fit for their project because you've worked with similar content or formats. Plus you've got the soft skills, that is the ability to work well with people, to wrap all this talent up in. And you also sound fairly sane to go with it. Believe me, from the CVs I've read, few people seem to manage to tick every box.

Imagine you are asked to pitch your idea for a documentary strand that broadcasts on a terrestrial channel at 8pm on a Thursday. Would you wait till the day before to write your proposal? Hopefully not. You'd do your research into the series, to see what ideas they like, the format of the shows, the kinds of themes they cover. You'd gather the material to support your idea, maybe shoot some test interviews, back-up your proposal with detailed information. You'd ask a few friends to take a look through, you'd re-read it and proof it before submitting. Production companies invest thousands of hours in this kind of work, to make sure they get commissioned.

In the same way, you need to give your CV thorough time and thought. You need to be able to write a draft, then set it aside and look again a day or two later. You should give it to friends and colleagues to see what they make of it. It is essential to proof read and check grammar, for example to ensure you've made the right choice between 'their', 'they're' and 'there'. Once you've got your core CV, you should be updating it every month or so, even when you're in a long-term contract. This ensures that by the end of the programme you're working on, you're ready to send your CV off for the next one. The reality is that like a garden in winter, there're far more interesting things to be doing than reviewing your CV, so it tends to get abandoned until you actually need to send it out.

You cannot underestimate the importance of your CV. There is so much competition in the creative marketplace that the hardest part is not performing well when you're in the interview for the job. If you've got to the stage where you're actually sat face-to-face with your potential new boss, you're probably down to good odds, with only five to ten other candidates still in the game. That's a relatively high chance of getting the gig.

The hardest part is actually surviving the cull of CVs that don't tick the right boxes to make it on to the interview shortlist. Your CV is competing with hundreds of others to stand out. And remember, the interview slots might be filled by the time the production manager has read the 44th CV. So if yours is the 45th, then you're out of luck. Your CV might not even get read. That's the harsh reality of winning short contract, freelance creative work, which makes it clear just how important it is to have an up-to-date, thought through and well-structured CV that communicates quickly and clearly, to bring you right into the mind of the person reading it.

The Clearly Creative process will give you the tools and understanding to help you to shape up your CV and get on to that interview shortlist.

Chapter 2

Who's reading your CV?

We've established that the purpose of your CV is to give your potential employer that perfect First Moment of Truth. It must show off what you've done and what you know, presenting your experience and training in a formal and favourable way that will get them to pick you off the shelf and put you into their shopping trolley.

However, many people make a key mistake right at the beginning when writing their CV. They think of every single job they've done. Everything they've learned. All the certificates and badges they've won. And somehow try and squeeze it all in. They're broadcasting in full HD everything that they think needs to be known about them.

Only this isn't where a broadcaster starts when they're making a television programme. No programme gets commissioned without some knowledge of the audience. TV stations monitor viewing figures like a hawk. They track interaction on websites and social media. They commission audience research. They look at what is popular with the demographic who watch that channel in that time slot in order to commission programmes that fit that demographic rather than finding a market for their new programme.

Have you researched who your audience is for your CV?

The first thing you have to ask yourself is 'Who's actually reading my CV?' To be honest, you probably won't know. Sometimes it's the producer on the project, or the office manager. Sometimes it's a production assistant who's been instructed to go through the hundreds of applications and do an initial cull of the CVs submitted. There are some generalisations you can make about them, though, so you can put yourself in their shoes.

Time Poor

Producers and production managers are responsible for getting the show made. They've got budgets to prepare for the Executive Producer to sign off. They've got hazard assessment forms to review before the call sheet can go out for Saturday's show. They've got invoices to double-check for payment. Oh, and they have to recruit a camera man and an editor for a documentary that's starting to film in two weeks' time, which has finally been given a green light after eighteen months of development. Recruiting for these roles is just another line to add to their long list of tasks for today.

Inundated

Having placed a job ad, probably online, they're now being inundated with candidates. The Internet has made applying for jobs quick and easy, which means people can apply for multiple jobs indiscriminately in minutes, clogging up inboxes. That doesn't necessarily mean you've got a lot of competition, since many of those applicants will be unsuitable, but they're only going to spend moments initially looking at your CV.

Experienced

These people have reached a position of influence through hard work and experience. When they read your CV they'll be able to suss you out pretty quickly. Simply by looking at the programmes and the roles you've done they'll know what you're capable of. Or more accurately, they'll have an 'idea' of what you're capable of, even though you may have worked beyond the job title.

Responsible

Employers are responsible for fulfilling recruitment policies. Some of these will be requirements set down in law, some of these will be determined by company policy, some may be informal. However, they have to make sure they conform to legislation on hours and rates. They have to make sure that you're insured. They may need to make sure you're trained in certain skills before you can join the production. And they also have to ensure that you are legally entitled to work in the country that the production is taking place in.

Human

Finally, remember that they're human. You never know what frame of mind they'll be in when they're reading your CV. They might be just back from a crafty lunchtime pint for someone's birthday, or they could have just had a row with their partner on the phone over who's cooking dinner tonight. They might have had their budget cut and their delivery deadline shortened. You don't know what their attention span is, or what factors will affect it. So you need to make sure that your CV is clear, concise, to the point, and leaves no ambiguity or reason for doubt.

How They Read your CV

We carried out a Clearly Creative survey, to put our theories to the test and find out more about the way the producers and production managers went about recruiting. We asked employers if they read submitted CVs on screen or printed them out. The result was quite remarkable. Just 7% printed them out on paper. That leaves the vast majority, 93% who will read your CV on their computer screen. What are the implications for the way you approach your CV?

Well, two key things. The first is you need to layout your CV with screen viewing in mind, but I'll talk about this later in Chapter 7 - Structure. Second, though, it shows that your CV is in competition with many other things going on at the same time. While they're reading about the documentary you made exposing child labour exploitation on the other side of the world, an email alert is telling them the studio they pencilled needs to be confirmed or they'll lose it to another production, an Assistant Producer is chatting to them on Skype about a music track they want cleared… and that's before you get to phone calls, Facebook pinging, the tea round…

You need your CV to be attention-deficient proof, so your potential employer is able to scan it in just twenty seconds, and be sufficiently enticed that they will give it their full concentration before their attention is required elsewhere. You must have a sharp and well-baited hook that they are enticed to give you their full attention.

Chapter 3

Selling yourself

If you're working in the television, film, advertising or design industries, you're almost certainly a creative individual. You want to make great insightful documentaries that will open people's minds or tell stories of romances in far away places. Maybe you want to entertain them on a Saturday night, make them laugh, gasp and cry.

Even if you're in a production role, you'll still have a creative heart. The last thing you want to be doing is working in a retail. Pah, you were last working in a sales environment while at University, either stacking shelves, pulling pints or selling shoes.

Ask yourself how do you get your creative work? As you get more experience and build up your contacts, the work will hopefully come to you as people recommend you for jobs. That is unlikely to work every single time you're looking for a contract. There are production companies out there who are in the market for someone with the skills you have, but do you honestly think they are just going to knock on your door?

Of course you know it's not that easy, so you'll have been sending out your CV, calling up contacts and joining job websites. Crass as it might sound, you've been selling yourself. Like a salesman in a used car yard, you've been drumming up trade for your skills. You've started to shout about your wares, or at least talking in a hushed voice about them. To do this with greater effectiveness you need to know a little bit about marketing.

When you're shopping, there are two modes of purchases. First, there's 'desire', where you make a purchase solely on your desire to own it. You might be in a clothes store, for example, and you see a great T-shirt and you think yeah, I don't need another T-shirt but this one with the pug on it is kind of fun, I'll buy it. Your decision is based on the desire to own the product. It does not fill a specific need or set of criteria that you established before you walked out of your front door to go shopping.

The other mode is 'need' shopping, when you are purchasing a specific item because you need it and you cannot be without that item. The methodology that you use when 'need' shopping is very different, you will have a list of performance factors that the product must fulfil for you to actually make that purchase.

For example, imagine you win a job which means you'll be filming in the Welsh mountainside in winter. You're going to need a new coat that will keep you warm and protect you from the elements. When you hit the shops, your criteria will be heavily influenced by practical factors like does the coat fit well, is it rainproof, and is it lined? When making your final decision, you'll still be influenced by desire, finding one which you think you look good in, but essentially you're fulfilling a need. You might not tick every single criteria, for example you might have set out to buy a coat with a hood. If the one you like most doesn't have one, you may well still buy the coat, but only if it satisfied enough of your other criteria to fulfil your need for a winter coat.

Recruiting for television production isn't about desire purchasing. No production manager idly browses for a researcher, just in case they see one they like the look of. They have to need a researcher to work on a specific project, they'll then set out with a shopping list of specific skills to find one. Just like the coat without the hood, they might set out to find one with experience of working on magazine shows, but find someone without that direct experience who ticks so many other boxes that they hire them anyway.

Your objective is simple then: make it easy for your potential employer to tick off their list of requirements quickly and simply. You can achieve this in the way that your buyer looks at you. Commercial organisations spend millions researching what influences consumers' purchasing decisions. By understanding these influencing factors, then applying them to your CV you can make sure they're more likely to take you to the checkout than other candidates. Here are some of the key influences on purchasing.

Product

Of course the product has to fulfil the desire or need. Whether it's a pair of handmade leather brogues costing £400 or a high street pair made in a factory and retailing for £40, they have to do the job that is required of them: fit properly and be comfortable to walk in. So, as a cameraman the product you sell is your ability to set up lighting, prepare the camera and then film great footage. For an editor, it's your knowledge of the editing software and your knack for cutting those rushes into a coherent sequence for the programme. If you're a Production Co-ordinator, it's your ability to write call sheets, book crew and manage the whole team.

While the job title will indicate a general area of expertise, there may be specific skills they're seeking for in a candidate, for example:

- can operate a Panasonic P2 HD camera
- has worked with children with sensitive issues
- can speak Spanish.

These requirements are sometimes included within the details of the job advert. They can also be hidden within the description of the show. If the ad is for a cameraman on a programme called 'High Risers: The World's Tallest Skyscrapers' they're probably not looking for someone with vertigo. However, there are some criteria that aren't apparent from the job ad. So, you need to make sure that your key skills are communicated so that they know you're the right product for the job, even when you don't know which skills they're looking for!

Availability

How does the consumer get hold of the product? Can they walk into any store and find it on the shelf? Or do they need to go to a particular brand store? Or perhaps order something bespoke online?

In the same way, how available are you? How can they contact you? How many job sites do they find you on? Or is your showreel only on your personal website? Can your contact details be found quickly and easily? If they Google your name, what will they find?

Service

Service is the way in which the product is delivered. Imagine ordering a meal in a fast food chain. Now visualise stepping into a Mayfair restaurant and being greeted by the Maitre D'. Of course the whole experience will be on a completely different level.

What quality of service do you deliver? Is it with a smile or a grimace? Is it an easy process to engage your services? Or is it made complicated by you not returning calls or responding to emails?

Value

Price, in itself, is not a key factor. What is more important is the value of the object. To some, a designer handbag at £2,000 seems preposterous. To others, to own a piece by that brand is worth the investment. Value is created through the perception of the purchaser.

A producer knows that a cameraman with twenty years' experience will command a higher day rate than a new entrant. They also know for that fee they'll get a better end result and probably at a quicker pace. So if they're after high quality images captured with speed and efficiency, the more experienced cameraman is better value. However, if it's just a test shoot and they only want basic footage from a static camera, then they'll get better value from a new entrant, who will get a basic job done and be cheap with it.

While you shouldn't mention your rates on your CV, an employer will be able to look through your CV and judge your rate. Or more accurately, they will calculate how much they are willing to pay you according to the job in hand and your level of experience. Making sure your CV expresses your skills and experience effectively will help the employer be more accurate in judging how much you're worth paying. Through my Clearly Creative techniques, I've helped freelancers add £5,000 per annum to their perceived value by doing just this.

Emotional Engagement

This is all about how the product makes you feel. A new pair of sunglasses can make you feel glamorous or cool. An organic smoothie can make you feel wholesome and counterbalance the cocktails you downed the night before.

When you work with people, how do you make them feel? Are you friendly? Ruthlessly ambitious? Difficult to talk to? Can't shut up? One turn off can be an overly eager CV, where someone is desperately trying to convince you they're right for the job (and I've been guilty of making such applications when I was starting out!). Getting a balanced emotional response to your CV is essential.

Consistency

A brand is at its strongest when your whole experience of that brand is consistent. My favourite example of this is the department store John Lewis, which for me has the most amazingly consistent brand experience. From their shops and their staff to their website and phone lines, they are consistent in their straightforward, quality but value approach. Their branding, whether it's the style of shop signage or their photography, is consistently classy, cool and inviting. Whether you're buying bed linen online, a television in store, or cooking with their Waitrose label food products, they have created a clear and distinct John Lewis brand experience.

What about you? Is your CV in the same font as your invoices? Is the format of your telephone number on your CV the same on your email signature? Does your voicemail message have the same figurative tone of voice as that of your CV?

These are the factors that influence employers when they are looking through your CV and trying to choose whether to take your application to the next stage. That influence may be very tangible, it may be subliminal. Either way, you need to make sure the shopping experience that your purchasers have with you is a positive one. As we go through the Clearly Creative process, I'll be explaining to you exactly how to do this.

Chapter 4

Visualising Your Career

I've found visualising change is an incredibly useful tool. There are various techniques, depending on what you're aiming to achieve, but the overarching concept is that when you want to make a change in your life, you visualise what that change will look like. This then helps you move towards that goal with greater chance of success.

At Napoleon Creative we wanted to revamp our website which was a few years old. We sat down, listed everything we wanted to tell potential new clients and then came up with a design. It looked very nice, but it was cluttered with links and information. It didn't feel quite right, so we parked it to one side for a week or two. Coming back to it, I realised that actually, the website was all about our anxieties as a company. We didn't want to put off any job, large or small. We wanted to offer every single service we could. We were screaming for attention, for someone to give us a chance to show what we know.

I sat with the designer and explained my observations. He agreed. So I said let's visualise the company in a year's time. We've moved to a bigger office (which was already in motion). We've won more work. We're doing more ambitious projects. We've got new clients. We're able to be more creative in the work we do. We looked at websites of the agencies we aspired to be like. The designer went away and came up with a brilliant new design. In our humble opinion, it exudes confidence, style and clarity. It looks like it belongs to the level of production company we wanted to lift ourselves towards. This was achieved only by visualising what we wanted to become, not by dwelling on what we feared as a production company.

Take a few minutes to think about your career right now. You might like to write some notes down on paper. What opportunities are available to you? How do you feel about your career prospects? What skills do you have to offer? How do you think people perceive you? How do you feel about stepping into that busy, creative market place?

Now put that piece of paper to one side. Imagine yourself in a year from now. You've won new work on the exact programme you want to work for. Your day rate has increased. You're spending less time between contracts. You have more contacts who are higher up in production, so can get you more leads for work. You've refined your CV to accurately express your skills. You know when you send out your CV that people are understanding your skills more clearly and are valuing you more highly. Write down how this makes you feel.

Now think of your CV. What does the version of the new you look like? What fonts does it employ? What kind of tone does it take? What paper is it printed on? You might even go as far as writing a fantasy CV of the work you've done in the year ahead, the career progression you've made in those twelve months.

This might sound like hocus pocus, but I promise you it works. Once you have that vision in your head, you'll be ready to start thinking about your CV in a fresh way, and then start making that vision become a reality with the Clearly Creative CV techniques.

Chapter 5

What kind of shop are you?

If, then, you're essentially a sales person, you'll need a place to sell from. A wide display table to lay out your range of skills, shelves on which to display your framed qualifications. So as part of your marketing plan, what is your shop going to look like? Where do you put up posters to advertise your store? Once inside, what is the look of your store? Is it exposed brick work and 1950s style shop fittings, or is it all white walls and gleaming chrome? Are you a small boutique tucked away down a side road, or are you proudly in the biggest mall in town?

When I ask this question at my workshops, attendees often come back with 'I'm a small shop, like a bespoke tailor. Where everything is made especially. I have a very one-on-one relationship with my customers.' Working in a creative field makes you feel like that, as you're often working in small teams, for a relatively short period of time in a 'hothouse' scenario. You pour your creativity into a project, and you tailor everything you do to it. You'll have one specific role, but you'll do your best for the production whatever you're asked.

Increasingly, crew are expected to be one-person filmmakers, able to research, shoot and edit footage all by themselves. With the explosion in digital media, they also work on a wider range of projects than ever before. I've been runner, researcher, cameraman, director, producer and occasionally make-up artist. I've worked on feature films, children's dramas filmed in studios, documentaries about Hollywood stars and the National Lottery Draw. I once spent an hour stroking puppies in Battersea Dog's Home so they didn't whine over the interview we were filming. I've worked on projects shot on 35mm, DigiBeta, full HD and Super 8. I've filmed in Knightsbridge mansions and in a sewerage plant in Cardiff. I've worked on websites, conference presentations, photo shoots, magazines articles and interactive TV applications.

As you progress through your career, you will build a wide array of skills and be exposed to many different production styles. You never know which of these is going to be the one that will get you the job. It might be your latest role. It actually might be three jobs ago because you worked with a particular presenter. Or it might be because tucked in there somewhere you reveal you speak Italian, and the job is going to be shot on the canals of Venice.

For this reason, you should think of your career as a department store. It's the big one, in the centre of town, spread over five storeys. You've got a clutch of qualifications in your education and training departments. You've got office and running experience stacked in boxes. There are bookcases lined with your research skills. A customer service desk looks after all your co-ordination skills. There's a whole floor devoted to technology, with a fantastic display of all the cameras you know how to use and the editing and effects software you've used. Then displayed on a series of mannequins are the various outfits you've worn while directing. One has a North Face puffer jacket and hiking boots you wore halfway up Ben Nevis, another the smart suit you wore when interviewing Alan Sugar, and in the front of the display one with the red tie ensemble you wore covering the red carpet at the BAFTA awards.

Now, this sounds like a great store, with everything a production manager could want when they come shopping. In fact, when they step inside the door of your department store, they're going to be downright bewildered. How will they know if you sell research skills? What about experience on chat shows? Is that near the make-up and perfumes? They might be looking for editing skills. Which floor are they on?

What they will need is a store directory, a prominent sign that combines text and graphics to quickly communicate the store's layout, departments and facilities. The store directory is particularly important for the customer who is shopping for a 'need' purchase. They want to walk in, glance at the directory and within a few seconds know whether the store has the product they're looking for, and where in the shop to find it. And yes, you can see where I'm going here… your CV needs to be that directory.

When someone picks up your CV, the experience should be like looking at a store directory. It must be clearly labelled, and immediately understandable from a distance. It needs to pass the scan test, where in twenty seconds they can pick up an idea of what skills you have to offer, that your editing skills are on the fourth floor and directing skills are on the fifth.

Next time you're in a large shop, look for the store directory. They will have spent a lot time and resources testing this for legibility and simple communication. Notice how they use colours, whether they stick to their brand colours or strip back to black and white. What kinds of fonts do they use, and in what weights? How do they present the information, are there lists of what's on each floor, or is it one long alphabetical list of departments with the location marked alongside? When you look at the directory, how does it feel? Can you scan quickly? Choose a random product, how long does it take to find out whether they sell it and if so where?

Look at your CV. Does it have the same impact? Does your eye scan it effortlessly? Can you easily see the various sections? Can you find information easily and simple? Well, the Clearly Creative process will help you achieve that. Now that you have that visual image of the store directory feel you're trying to achieve, it's time to begin.

PART 2:
Creating a Clearly Creative CV

Chapter 6

The Importance of Being Inert

At the start of our careers, a friend who had worked in marketing for the same company for two years asked for my advice. She'd applied for a new job with a different company and they'd made her an offer. While the money was better and she was a little bored in her existing role, she was suddenly nervous. What if she didn't like the new job? What if she didn't get the challenges she was looking for or the actual workload differed to the job description?

I pointed out to her that actually, in the time she'd worked for just one employer, I'd had three, and worked on seven or more different production teams. I'd worked short contracts of only a week and longer ones of three months. I learned pretty quickly that changing production teams teaches you new ways of working, different ways of thinking and meeting new people. So I told her to get out and try something new! She did, and loved the new working environment and the challenges that it brought.

So what has this got to do with your CV and being inert, which essentially means inactive? Well, if you're constantly looking for work, your CV will be passed in front of a lot of noses. In small companies, it is likely to be reviewed in a less formal way than it will within in a large organisation. There may be no formal Human Resources department or recruitment process, the shortlisting can be down to the whim of one person alone. You need to make sure that it creates the right reaction for that person.

Now, as I mentioned at the start of this book, the hardest challenge for your CV is not getting the right reaction to get shortlisted; it's not creating the wrong reaction. You never know what will make someone discard your CV. When the production manager is overwhelmed by choice, they are sometimes searching for a reason to discard your CV, simply to cull the numbers. It could be you went to a University they didn't rate based on hearsay from a friend. They might see your address and perceive you'd have to commute too far to the production office. Maybe they can't see how your experience matches what is on their 'need' list. These factors can be entirely arbitrary.

> Once I disregarded a CV because the applicant's showreel had a montage of shots with Eva Cassidy singing on it. I'm not a fan of Eva Cassidy's music. Having already watched quite a few showreels, I couldn't bring myself to listen to Eva, so skipped that application. I've even binned a CV simply because the applicant lived in Tooting Bec. It may well be a lovely place, but I think Tooting Bec is a silly name for somewhere to live. When going through a stack of CVs for a one-day job at 9.30pm after a glass of wine, it felt like a perfectly good reason to delete that CV off my list. Random, uncalled for discrimination but true.

And now a quick Chemistry lesson. An inert substance is one that has little or no ability to react with another chemical. However, it helps facilitate other chemical reactions, it just doesn't particularly join in the action itself.

Likewise, the CVs that stand out for me in terms of simple readability are the ones that are simple, factual and brief. The applicants use the details of their experience to communicate their skill level, rather than by using adjectives. Like an inert chemical, the CV facilities a reaction within the employer's mind, where they make their own judgment on the applicant's level of skill based on the facts put before them.

Next time you get home and there's a leaflet dropped on the door mat for a local non-chain pizza place, pick it up and look at it. It's likely to have stock images, clashing colours and bad spelling. Some CVs, particularly from younger crew, give exactly the same reading experience. They are incredibly eager and earnest, use emotive words like 'keen' or 'ambitious'. They include phrases like 'team player' and 'excellent with Z1 cameras'. This kind of enthusiasm can actually become really tiring to read and as an employer, you also become blind to it. Just like the pizza leaflet it ends up in the bin.

Next time you're walking past Pizza Express, look at the posters in the window, encouraging diners to take a seat at their table. The design will be simple, using clearly recognisable brand elements. The copy will be short, punchy and with a clear sales message. Sure, the marketing budget for creating the poster will be a hundred times higher than that of the local pizza place, but this is closer to impact that you're aiming to achieve with your CV.

There are some key places in your CV where you must try to be inert to reduce the risk of raising the hackles of your potential employer without realising it. By keeping the design of your CV simple, your language factual and being economical with adjectives, you will reduce the chance of a negative reaction to what you are writing. Your goal is to strip your CV of distractions, little bits of information that raise the tiniest doubt in the employer's mind, so they can concentrate solely on your skills and how appropriate you are for the job. I'll be pointing out what these are as we start to build the contents.

Chapter 7

Structure

In our survey, when we asked employers what was the most important element of a CV, unsurprisingly at the top of the list was skills with 40%. After all, that's the whole point of requesting a CV, so they have a document that outlines your professional capabilities.

Joint second came credits and layout, both with 20%. This shows that equal in importance with which programme you learned those skills on, is the presentation of those skills. So it's not just that you were a floor manager on Blue Peter, it's that they can find your floor managing skills clearly and easily.

They're not going to employ you if your skillset doesn't match their job description even if you've got an expertly laid out CV. They will thank you, however, if they can come to that decision quickly because your CV is well presented.

How Long?

Before we start getting into structure in detail, let's talk about how long your CV should be. Traditionally, CVs of people established in their career should be two pages. The strange thing is, they always have to be full pages. If I receive a CV where the second page is only two thirds full it looks funny. Funny odd, not funny ha ha.

Imagine opening a newspaper and seeing a full-page advert. Then you notice they've only put images and copy in two thirds of the page and the bottom section is left completely blank. Wouldn't that look odd? They've paid for the space, but they're not using it? Has someone at the newspaper forgotten to place another ad below it?

When you look at a CV, if there's a gap at the bottom, it looks like you've run out of things to say. Even if you don't have anything to say it's better to space our your content so it evenly fills two pages. Strange but true.

If you're just starting out in your career, don't feel obliged to fill two pages. You'd be better off having a single page CV that is selective and only details relevant work experience, than listing your paper round and every single GCSE you passed.

Having a one-page CV as a junior member of crew is like saying 'hey, I don't have much experience, but I recognise that, and know I have a lot to learn before I can fill two pages.' If you're incredibly established, and you're directing top TV shows, then your CV may also be only one page, since the list of shows will be instantly recognisable and will speak for itself.

As mentioned previously, we get through a lot of jobs in our creative careers and if we wrote detailed descriptions of each one, our CVs would be over five pages long. In fact, a cameraman who approached me to help him with his CV and online presence had just that. Five pages of different jobs, some a single day, some a week long. He didn't want to leave any job out, in case his experience filming at the top of Nelson's Column or filming multiple camera music shoots was the exact thing that the new employer was searching for.

I went through the CV with him. We grouped experiences into themes, putting his music jobs together, his news work in another section and so on. We culled the list of jobs and just picked really stand-out shoots, like the ones above. Before long we'd got the CV down to two concise, punchy pages. Any employer reading it would know there were many more shoots, but the experience he had was clear, without having to read through five pages to do so.

We'll go into this in more detail later in the Clearly Creative process, but having established the one or two full pages rule, you now need to set that aside. When you're writing your CV you should simply write. Following the rules we're going to establish below, just write as clearly and concisely as possible. You might end up with three or even four pages. When you've got the content you feel you need, then it's time to edit this down to two pages, which I'll cover later.

Layout

The Curriculum Vitae has a distinct format or layout. There are key areas which CVs should have, since every employer, regardless of the industry, will want to know these facts. They should be laid out in this priority:

Header
Personal Introduction
Work History (Credits)
Training / Education
Hobbies and Interests
References

Now let's begin!

Chapter 8

Header

Your Name and Role

You're walking along the local high street, past a row of shop windows, each jostling for a bit of your attention and some quality time with your credit card. How much does the brand name stand out on the shop front? How can you tell what they do? For any major high street brand this will be clear and distinct.

Your CV needs to have the same kind of instant impact on the reader. Think of your name as the brand of your store. Right at the top, a clear declaration of who you are in the biggest font to appear on the CV so they can identify your name.

When someone sends me a CV where their name is in the same font, weighting and colour as the body text, then often I don't even see it. I skip straight to the body copy. You need to highlight your name so that when they're reading your CV, your name fixes in the reader's brain. Then, if they spot something that they like about you and want to go back to your CV later, they're more likely to recall your name and be able to find your application.

When you're walking along the high street, there's not doubt what the majority of shops sell, after all they fill their windows with it! Furniture shops have sofas and chairs, fashion retailers have mannequins with clothes on, health food shops have displays of vitamin bottles. Your CV doesn't have an equivalent visual cue to say what you do, unless you include a photograph of you holding an appropriate piece of equipment, but even that can be misleading (I advise not putting your photograph on your CV, but more of that later). In fact, some of the CVs I see have a person's name but nothing to tell me what role they perform. I have to start reading through to find out what they do. An empty window display is hardly going to lure passing trade to cross the threshold, is it?

Imagine a production manager is crewing three roles to start in a fortnight's time, one of which you're perfect for, plus say an editor and a camera person. Their assistant has culled the applications and printed out the most suitable ones. Unfortunately, he trips while carrying the stack of CVs to the production manager's desk, scattering them over the floor. How easy is it to quickly work out from your CV which role you are applying for?

As you don't have a shop window, you need to have a clear and distinct way of saying what it is you do. Your job role should be placed confidently underneath your name, preferably in a font size smaller than your name, but larger than the body text. Ideally, your job title will match the one in the job application exactly. Here's what it should look like:

> Lewis Darby
> Animator
>
> Rebecca Muller
> Production Co-Ordinator
>
> Robin Thomas
> Self-Shooting Producer/Director

Accessibility

Within the Header you should also add your accessibility information, the ways the employer can get hold of you directly or the places where they can see more of your work. First, your mobile number. Don't put a landline, most potential employees will always go for your mobile first anyway. Putting the international dialling code prefix +44 isn't entirely necessary, unless you know that the employer is based outside the UK.

You should also include your email address, which should be clearly related to your name. This is where you can show consistency. If your name is Rebecca, but everyone calls you Becky, and your email is BeckyMuller@cv4.tv then call yourself Becky on your CV.

A playful email address like gordonthecameraman@cv4.tv is perfectly acceptable, as long as it refers to something related to your career. Rudeboy@cv4.tv just doesn't cut it professionally. If your email isn't easy to read because it features numbers or initials which are only meaningful to you, you should consider changing it. Your potential employer needs to be able to type that email address quickly and easily. If they're trying to type in grnnbch@cv4.tv and they miss out the second 'n' and get a bounce back, they might not bother trying to email you again. This might mean you have to set up two email accounts, one for work, one for personal use, which while an inconvenience can also have benefits (see Chapter 24 - Social Media).

Next you should have a link to your showreel or website, if appropriate for your role. This needn't be a whole dedicated website, it might simply be your Vimeo profile. Be sure, however, to give yourself a dedicated URL, so for example ours is www.vimeo.com/napoleon (search their help forum for how to do this). To be absolutely clear, though, for roles like cameraman, director, editor, animator, set designer and make-up artist a showreel is essential. In today's world where so much media content is just one click away, there's no reason not to have one. I've had camera people apply for jobs with nothing but their word to say they can light something. When you're in competition with applicants who have their own sites with all their work available at a click or two away, not having a showreel sends you off the pitch straight without having touched the ball. If you can't get hold of copies of your work, it's often available online anyway.

> One cameraman I was interested in working with had no showreel, but with a few search words typed into YouTube I managed to find the programme he'd shot. You don't want to rely on your potential employer being willing to do the same. More and more broadcasters and production companies are making shows available online. It might be a simple case of setting up a YouTube playlist of material posted by others.

You also want to list any profiles you might have on job sites like Production Base or LinkedIn. LinkedIn is important as with one click it can show employers the contacts that you have in common, which might lead to a quick and effective reference for you. If you're using Twitter in a way that's appropriate for work, you might want to add that too. If your list of links is starting to look cluttered you could amalgamate them on a site like www.about.me. I like this site because it has a simple, elegant look, here's mine www.about.me/gavinricketts

The Header must solve all your problems with accessibility. It should give the person looking at your CV easy direct contact with you, plus access to see your work and your other presences on the internet.

Photo

Studies have shown that adding your photo to your business card can greatly improve recall of who you were and what you did, which leads to greater sales. When I've met someone in person at a networking event, having a photo of them either on their business card or LinkedIn profile is useful to aid my memory and entirely appropriate. When I've not met a job applicant before, for me it's inappropriate to include a photo on the first piece of information I have from them, namely their CV. When confronted with a photo, I take in the way they look, the way they dress, where the photo is taken, how good the camerawork is. Involuntarily I'm making assumptions about them, which are more to do with aesthetics and their style and fashion brand preferences than they are about the person's skills. I find this distracting, I want to make a judgement on their abilities, not whether I like what they're wearing.

Having said that, I confess to occasionally letting photos influence my selection. I had to choose a runner to help us round up people to interview on the street as part of a video survey. It's hard to choose runners, because with little experience there's not much to differentiate them. After a chat with three of the applicants on the phone, I confess that when it came to picking from them, what swayed me was one of them had a photo. I thought that if she approached me in the street, I would not feel intimidated or threatened, but would give her my attention for a few moments.

When we needed an animator, a couple of CVs stood out. When I looked at one applicant's showreel on Vimeo, which was impressive, I saw from his photo that he had an armful of tattoos and piercings on his nose and ears. This isn't my style, I hate wearing jewellery, it irritates me. I stopped buying watches because I kept taking them off halfway through the day and losing them. The idea of piercings makes me itch. You might think, then, that his appearance went against him, but his look was so different from the people we had on the project team, I actively hired him because I wanted to add a different flavour of creative energy to the mix. However, I made that decision after I'd seen his CV and showreel, and had made an assessment of his talent as an animator.

It's likely that once your potential employer has read your CV, they'll come across your photo, for example if you've used one as your avatar on your Vimeo page. However, I strongly advise leaving your photograph off your CV. Let them read your CV first, and made a judgement of your skills before they respond to the way you look.

Date of Birth

I'm often surprised by applicants who put their full date of birth on their CV, even older crew members. It is illegal to discriminate on grounds of age. In fact, as an employer you have to word job adverts carefully. You can no longer, for example, advertise for a 'young runner'. Someone in their fifties could still do the job of a runner equally as well as someone in their twenties, so you are not allowed to limit applicants to being 'young'.

For the younger crew member, age doesn't really give any bearing on your maturity. I've worked with mature 18 year olds, and naïve 25 year olds. I advise excluding your age or date of birth, since a production manager reading your CV will get a sense of your age from your level of experience anyway. You need to let your maturity speak through your tone of voice when writing your CV.

At the other end of the age range spectrum, older crew members hide their age for being perceived to be too old. While it is illegal to discriminate on age, I'm sure it happens even if just subconsciously. In this highly competitive market, older crew can be perceived to command higher wages and have more time constraints, such as family commitments. You can also be seen as a dinosaur, out of touch with modern trends.

One of the first people I recruited was in, I'd guess, his fifties and I chose him for the job because he had the most experience out of all the people who applied, and particular expertise in news. As a relatively inexperienced director at the time, I felt that I was going to be in safe hands, since this was going to be a news style piece at a big and very busy motor show. The cameraman was indeed experienced, but he was also set in his ways. I didn't like the visual style he was shooting in and he gave me shots I knew I didn't need. No matter how much I tried to direct him, he was always off getting what he thought was the best shot. Now, his inability to take direction wasn't a trait exclusive to those over forty, but the experience did put me off hiring older crew for a few shoots.

When an older, more experienced member of crew applies for a more junior position, it piques my interest. Are they just out of a contract and are filling in time? Or are they finding work is running out? I've had the experience of employing people who are way overqualified, who are ultimately professional, take the money but make it clear that they're doing it at a cut rate.

Sometimes, the project actually calls for older crew. I had a project where I was interviewing the very top guy of a large multinational organisation. I'd filmed this guy before. He probably bills in the thousands of pounds an hour bracket. You get five minutes of his time. He sits, you have about two minutes to tweak the lights, then he says what he wants to say. You get to make one or two comments to direct his performance, he says a few more words, then leaves for his next meeting. For any job when you're interviewing someone at that level within an organisation, you need a mature cameraman, someone who knows what they're doing and can light quickly and efficiently. You also want someone who is able to charm the guy but not be intimidated by him. In my opinion you only build this kind of maturity through age.

To avoid all this complication over the perceptions of your age if you are older, leave your birth date off and drop the graduation year from education listing, so you can remain inert. Employers will be able to guess your age within a few years, but without an exact age there is one less piece of information to distract from your skills.

Deeper understanding
Long-term collaboration
Developed over several years
Appreciate discretion

Address

Stating where you live is an equally awkward issue. Perception of distance from the office can be a powerfully influential factor, especially if you're going to be filming for a length of time in a particular location. If your home is near the production office, then this can be helpful, since you should be able to get to work easily and quickly.

> For short jobs, I have disregarded CVs because the applicant is not based in a location close to that day's filming. I had a one-day job where I'd whittled down the candidates to two people. They had equal experience, charging slightly different rates. However, one was based in Brighton and he expected his train fare to be covered. The shoot was at 9am, so it was going to be quite an expensive ticket. Okay, not a huge fare by any means, but still an additional expense. Also in my brain was the fact that he's coming by train, how reliable is that, what if he gets stuck in Sussex, he's not going to be able to simply grab a cab. In the end, I went with the London-based candidate for the sake of simplicity.
>
> On the other hand, I'd once filtered an animator role down to a few candidates. When it got to the interview stage, there was one stand out candidate. Great animation work. I had an initial telephone conversation with him, he had a good polite manner. Clearly articulate. During the interview it occurred to me that I didn't know where he was living. It transpired that his home was in Farnborough. Having lived out of London in that direction, I knew what a painful commute that could be on occasion. However, I was so convinced by his abilities that I thought, hey, the commute is his stress, not mine.
>
> By leaving off his address, he took the issue of his address completely off my mind until I'd made a judgement of his skills. I got him for a week to see how things went. Three years later he's still working for me, still commuting, and still at his desk by 9am every morning.

My advice is to either leave off your address or simply state a general idea of locality, like 'London-based'. This can cover living in Camden, a few streets from MTV's studios, or way out in Croydon. Anyway, it can take as long to commute from one end of Zone 2 to the other, as it can to take the train from Guildford to Waterloo for LWT's studios.

Employers will not throw away your CV simply on the basis of your location. However, it is an influence. When as a purchaser you have a wide choice of products, you need a criteria to whittle down your selection. At least if you make your CV as inert as possible and strip away those little details that cast doubt in the reader, you're being selected for your skills, which if good enough, if appropriate enough, will outweigh any detail like age or location.

Chapter 9

Personal Introduction

As I've already noted, employers are most likely to read your CV on screen. This means whether they're reading them in Word, a web browser or on a PDF viewer, they're likely to see only the top third of the page to begin with. That makes this the most important plot of your CV's real estate. Given that the top 15% of the page will already be taken up with the header, you need to make sure that what you include in the rest of that space has high impact.

You never know what part of your experience will interest an employer. It might be that you've worked on a particular format for a show earlier on in your career, which doesn't feature till the second page. This is where the Personal Introduction comes in, which should be the first thing that an employer reads. It's a summary of the key skills you have, your experience and your aspirations. And it's a maximum of two paragraphs. Maybe three at a push. Think of it as a trailer for the feature that is your career so far.

Wait, hold on, how many trailers have you seen where they're a mish-mash of all the best bits of the movie, cut into an incoherent sequence, which when you get to the cinema, bear no resemblance to the mess of a film you sit though for two hours?

A better way of thinking about it is as a news article. A good journalist will include all the essential details of a story in the opening few lines, so the reader knows the basic elements of the story. However, they'll also try pique your interest in those first few sentences so you'll keep reading.

When writing your Personal Introduction, you need to make sure you stick to the principles of being inert to make sure that it reads simply, clearly and communicates without boasting.

As with the header, in the first line of your CV you should positively reinforce the role that you take within a production. There's nothing worse than a wishy-washy 'I'm a multi-skilled filmmaker'. Well, no, the job advert was for an editor. Not a filmmaker. As with the header, make sure you confidently state the role in which you consider yourself a practitioner.

Too many CVs have overbearing personal statements, filled with clichés and unquantifiable phrases that leave you with no real sense of the person. Let's take an often-used word as an example: 'experienced'. It sounds an obvious word to used within a CV. You want to show that you have gathered real skills through your working life. But how do you actually quantify how much experience makes you 'experienced'? Does it mean two years? Fifteen years? And let's say you're an 'experienced producer/director'. Okay, but how have you gathered that experience? What kind of shows do you have experience of?

To quantify your experience, you simply need to give your description concrete years and formats, rather than adjectives. Try this simple phrase:

> I am a producer with seven years experience, working mainly on film documentaries and chat shows.

That way the reader knows straight away what you do, how long you've done it, and where you gained your experience. Putting it in the present tense solidly confirms that this is what you actively do for a living and because it's completely factual, it cannot be disputed. If this fits with the employer's vision of their ideal candidate, they will read on.

Breadth and Depth

In the body of your Personal Introduction, and also as you start to populate your credits list with details, you need to communicate across two axes: the depth and the breadth of your experience.

Depth of experience is when you know a particular kind of programme or style of filming in great detail, and you've had an extended amount of experience with it. So for example, you might have spent two years working on a TV series that broadcasts two 13 episode blocks a year. That means within that two-year period you've done 52 episodes. You'll know that format inside out. Say you spend three series on the BBC's

Watchdog, clearly you'll know the magazine format back to front, plus a knowledge of working with legal restrictions.

Breadth of experience is the wide range of scenarios which you've worked in. Whether that's because you've jumped from one kind of show to another, or because the challenges on one show were very varied, you're trying to get across that you've done a little bit of everything. You might have spent two months on a studio show; three weeks on a short corporate shoot, and then worked on an archive-based documentary. If you're a cameraman, you want to show the wide range of circumstances under which you've lit and shot.

After your positive statement about your role and years of experience, in the next few sentences of your Personal Introduction go into further details about the programmes you like working on, and the different working environments you've worked in.

> When I was a researcher on television documentaries, my challenges were mainly to find obscure footage, preferably for little or no cost. When I was writing up my CV, I tried to give a flavour of the different materials I'd tracked down and cleared for broadcast. I picked the interview Woody Allen did for Playboy magazine back in 1967. I tracked a copy down, got the relevant permissions, and we featured the pictures on the show. Thankfully, Woody kept his clothes on in the photo spread.
>
> For another programme about science fiction, we were looking for some footage of astronauts in zero gravity. I contacted NASA who have a huge resource of copyright-free material. As I was spooling through the tape, I found a bizarre sequence where the astronauts took frogs out of containers and let them float in zero gravity. The poor things were kicking their legs with vigour but couldn't understand why their webbed feet wouldn't propel then through the air, even though they were floating like they did in water. The director of the show loved the shots, and they were thrown into the programme.
>
> In my personal introduction, I used these contrasting examples when describing the kinds of materials I worked with:

> I have worked with a wide range of copyright material (from Woody Allen posing for Playboy to frogs in space courtesy of NASA).

The great thing with these examples is that they put very strong images in the reader's mind. 'Woody Allen', ' Playboy', 'Frogs' and 'Space' all trigger visual reactions. One example is a still/photo, the other is moving footage, showing that I'm aware of copyright issues facing both these formats. There's also the technical requirements to get them into the programme, filming the magazine in a rostrum studio and arranging the standards conversation from NSTC to PAL. Suddenly you can see the breadth and depth of challenges I've faced.

Try to avoid emotive language and hollow clichés; the worst culprit is 'I can work independently or as part of a team'. It's in pretty much every recent graduate CV that I've read, so stating it by itself has become nearly meaningless. You need to validate the claim with examples of how you have worked as an individual and as a team. So try something like 'I've worked by myself, such as when I self-shot a documentary about teen mums, but I'm also happy working in a team, like when I worked on a game show for Channel 4.' That way you've qualified your claim.

Colouring Your CV

CVs can be a pretty dull, sterile read with lots of flat statements. I can read someone's whole CV and not have a single image in my mind of what this person's working life looks like. I suggest you learn to 'colour' your CV. I'm encouraging you to add visual images to your CV in order to bring your experience to life in the mind of the reader. Let's take an example:

> I'm an editor with extensive experience with Final Cut Pro through to broadcast standard.

That doesn't really tell me a lot. I can see an iMac on a desk, since FCP is an Apple product. I'm imagining that the editor maybe finishes off the programmes in a broadcast-level online suite. Maybe he works in an office, then attends an edit in a facilities house for broadcast. There's not a whole lot of detail there.

Now try this version:

> I'm an editor with four year's experience working mainly on weekend entertainment shows, like X Factor and Dancing on Ice.

Straight away, I'm seeing the editor sat in a suite, colourful images on the screens. Knowing the kinds of budgets and scale of production that these shows have, I know he's not sat on a laptop in a small production office. He's sat in a big suite, with high turnaround show pressure. I'm seeing people singing, people dancing and importantly I'm seeing the editor bring that all together to create Saturday night bliss. He's in a team of other editors and some animators, probably working with multiple directors during the week, each working on different parts of the programme. Compare this to:

> I'm an editor with two year's experience cutting programmes on rich teens swapping lives with poor teens from other countries for BBC3.

You're thinking of a different pace of editing, different kinds of footage to work with, a different kind of story telling. You're imagining a small office, perhaps even just working off a laptop as the building of the story is more important than the graphics and music. He's probably working with just one director, with input from the producer.

Factual descriptions like this take the production manager reading your CV out of their own desk and plonks them right next to you while you're working. If you can keep this principle of adding colour as you write your CV, you'll find it communicates not just the factual information, but lets the reader build an image of the skills you have and how you developed them.

Let's take an example from the personal introduction of someone who attended one of my Clearly Creative workshops:

> I have much experience producing and editing a number of short films, promos and commercials and aspire to working creatively & technically on film & television projects involving documentary & news broadcasters, as well as comedy and drama.

Look at the ambiguity in the first statement. See how weak the 'much' is, it's undefined, unclear and doesn't sound like a heck of a lot of experience. How many is a 'number' of short films? He presumed it like it sounded like quite a lot, but to me it sounds like not that many. Short films always sound like self-funded or student productions, so it sounds like he doesn't have that many professional credits. He 'aspires' to work creatively and technically; does this mean he doesn't work creatively now? Is his work dull and boring at the moment, he just has ambitions of being creative? Oh, and on a side note, I hate ampersands, I only use them in names, like Jones & Sons.

The list of projects he wants to work on - comedy, drama, news, documentary, film and television - sounds desperately unfocused. These are the aspirations of someone who just wants to work in media without any real discernment in the direction they want their career to go.

We sat down and talked about the work he did. I asked a few questions about his work and his aspirations, and gradually my understanding of his experience deepened. Following some work with me, he rephrased the opening lines of his Personal Statement:

> I am a Final Cut Pro Editor who has cut commercials and virals for a wide range of big name brands and agencies in Britain, Europe and the USA. I really enjoy cutting virals as they offer more creative freedom. They give me a chance to experiment with slightly longer edits such one that allowed me to imitate the rapid editing style from one of my favourite TV shows 'The Thick Of It'. I have a big interest in documentary, comedy, news and current affairs.

Straight away, the opening statement is clearer and more confident. He confirms the software he has knowledge of and what he likes about his job. There's a clear sense of pride and passion in what he does, without using any emotive language. By choosing the example of 'The Thick of It', suddenly his interests in comedy, news and current affairs makes sense, because the show is a combination of all three, shot in a faux documentary style.

This way of employing language that I'm recommending as part of the Clearly Creative process takes a while to perfect, but when you get it right, people aren't being given a hard sell, they're reading facts about you and come to their own conclusions about your abilities.

The Future

With the Personal Introduction, I also find it interesting when people include a sentence or two about the direction that they'd like their career to grow. Maybe they're working on a documentary of their own or they have aspirations to work on a particular kind of programme. It's nice to see a little personal ambition, and a recognition that they still have things to learn in the industry.

Chapter 10

Credits

The credits section is the core of your CV, where you list the programmes or projects you've worked on. To be honest, no matter how well you write your opening statement, it's your previous credits that your employer will probably look at first. After all, they're trying to recruit you for a project that has a format, a presenter, a channel to broadcast on and a time slot. They really want to see how your experience aligns with their project so they'll scan down your credits and look at the headings for each entry. If they quickly recognise what they're reading as suitable for the job in hand, they'll then go back and start reading your Personal Introduction.

Sadly, presenting the credits in a clear, simple way is where many crew members get it wrong. They're so keen to impress with the project they've worked on, they put the name of the programme first, something like this:

Breakfast News, BBC1, Assistant Producer

After all, they've worked for BBC1, the world's second largest employer in television (only surpassed by China's mass media). Its highly respected news department is relied on to report on the events that count as they happen. You've worked in that environment, doesn't that show your calibre?

Yes, of course it does. However, if you list the broadcaster first, you'll fail the scan test. Scan your eyes down the list below in literally two seconds:

Breakfast News, BBC1, Assistant Producer

Sky News, Sky Television, Assistant Producer

Sky News, Sky Television, Researcher

ITN News, ITN, Researcher

ITN News, ITN, Floor Runner

North West Tonight, BBC, Production Runner

At a quick glance, all you take in is a list of broadcasters. You don't see the career progression because your eye needs to work to actually find the job title on the line. This is why I recommend listing your credits with the Role first in bold for greater emphasis, then Title of the Programme, then Production Company like this:

Assistant Producer, Breakfast News, BBC1

Assistant Producer, Sky News, Sky Television

Researcher, Sky News, Sky Television

Researcher, ITN News, ITN

Floor Runner, ITN News, ITN

Production Runner, North West Tonight, BBC

That way, when prospective employers scan down your CV they'll quickly see your career progression, how you've moved up the production ladder, gaining experience as you go. This will immediately build their confidence in your abilities.

If you've worked for one company for a year, but worked on different projects, do list each of the productions as a separate job.

Dates

For each job list the date after the production company, ideally with no gaps so it appears that you've never been out of work. Certainly, you can work for just a week for a company and put down 'July 2010' as the date, implying you worked there for four weeks or so. This is permissible, but please don't exaggerate too much. If you get into the interview and have to confess to only having done a week's work not a month's, you'll look foolish.

I've had the experience of being contacted for a reference by a co-ordinator, who'd helped out on one leg of a long foreign shoot. We'd already filmed in India before she arrived, arranged by a co-ordinator with specific experience setting shoots up there. The new co-ordinator joined us because she had specific experience in the Far East, and she set up our filming in China, Vietnam and Philippines. However, when the call for a reference came, her potential new employer asked me about the three months work she'd done across India and the Far East. What was I to say? She certainly hadn't worked that long, and didn't do any of the India co-ordination. She's done a great job on the Far East part of the shoot and I talked favourably about that. I avoided mentioning India at all. This might have been a misunderstanding with her new employer during the interview, but it put me in an awkward position. By all means be generous with the truth, but be warned it can come back to bite you.

Descriptions

Underneath the job title line, you need to give a brief description of the programme. There are hundreds of hours of programming broadcast every day, so unless you've worked on a flagship, headline-grabbing show like The One Show or Time Team, don't assume your employer will know the programme. This is especially important with satellite channel programmes, where not everyone has free access to the programming. A short synopsis will make clear what kind of show it was:

> This film review show was based on short packages about the week's cinema releases, followed by reviews by the presenter. Guest films stars were also interviewed.

> A studio-based debate show where guest celebrities argued over the day's headlines.

Now that you've established the format and content of the show, you need to tell them a short story of what you did on the show, building images inside the reader's head. You should put details that will enable the production manager to see you in action.

I was responsible for the celebrities on the show, from coming up with ideas for topical guests, to booking them via their agents, to settling them in their dressing rooms for the studio record.

I filmed in the homes of an extended family, who all lived on the same terraced street in Liverpool.

Combining the show's format with a few images that tell of the production will leave a clear idea of the programme in the reader's mind.

Beyond The Call

When providing details about the work you did on a particular show, remember this shouldn't be a job description. You don't need to explain to the Production Manager what you should have been doing all along. To stand out, you need to show how you added value to the production or went beyond your role.

These 'added value' achievements may be creative, technical or logistical. For example, completing an animation on time and on budget is par for the course for an animator. Introducing three new presets to a project and combining them into a completely new animation style is outstanding. As a production co-ordinator, booking equipment is expected of you. Negotiating a 30% discount for all kit hired or securing the first camera with a brand new technology to reach UK shores is really achieving something. As a director, interviewing a politician may be part of the job, but persuading her to exclusively reveal her true feelings about the party leadership is creating standout content for the programme.

Identify where you went above and beyond the call of duty, outside your job description, and include it in your credit. Sometimes it's hard to see these for yourself, as trying to achieve the best you can will be second nature to you, so do ask for feedback from your employers. Which of your achievements particularly stood out for them?

Truncating your Credits

Going back to the cameraman I mentioned earlier, here's how we truncated his experience. He'd divided up his experience into genres. For example, his news section originally looked like this:

News & Current affairs		
prod co.	**production**	**format**
(I work for all of these clients frequently)		
DAYBREAK	Entertainment/Showbiz/Features/ Live Premieres	DVCAM
BFBS TV	News, pieces to camera, reports for Armed Forces	XD cam
TF1 (French TV)	News/Interviews/Features	P2/DVC Pro
BBC Politics Show	Interview with key politicians	DV Cam
Reuters TV	Work For International Clients, (Greek / Jap)	DV Cam
ZDF (German TV)	Reports/Arts/Lifestyle/Fashion /Music	P2
Channel 4 News	News/Features/Business/ Music/Art	DVC PRO
Sky News	Lives/Recorded Packages/	P2
ITN	National News Reports / Lives / Packages /	DVCAM
CNBC	Financial/City Interviews/ 2 Camera Set Ups	BETA SP
London Tonight	Local News/Features/Reports/	DVCPro-
BBC London	News / Features / Studio Camera	DVC Pro
BBC News	Commons/Lives-Downing Street/Intvws	DV Cam

And the list continued. While that's an impressive selection of broadcasters, it does nothing to put images in your head as to what he's filmed. So we condensed it to this:

News & current affairs
I cover news stories for BBC Panorama, ITV Daybreak, BFBS (British Forces' TV), Sky News, TF1 (leading French broadcaster), ZDF, BBC Westminster, CNBC, APTN and Channel 4 News. I shoot on DV Cam, Digibeta, P2, or XD Cam. Stand out stories for me have been:

- shooting with political correspondents from across the channels on huge stories such as the July 7th bombings
- spending a day with Thierry Henry, the Arsenal footballer, showing a young fan round the Emirates Stadium.
- climbing to the top of Nelson's Column, for its 30 year refurbishment, for ITV London Tonight, and seeing fantastic views of the city
- flying to an exclusive spa resort in the Maldives with Coleen Nolan for ITV's This Morning
- filming many, many red carpet interviews and meeting the greats such as De Niro, Pacino, Winslett, Depp.

While both versions show the breadth and depth of his experience in a factual way, it's the second version where you visualise the work he's done. The short list of stand out stories puts clear images in your mind of the circumstances he's filmed in, from the top of Nelson's Column to the beaches of the Maldives.

Active Language

Another thing to note with this example, is the way I suggested he start the paragraph. He writes 'I cover news stories for…' This is what he does for a living, not 'I have in the past'. It's confident, active language. When choosing language, try and make the words as 'active' as possible. Here are some good words:

Pitched
Developed
Led
Instigated
Won
Scheduled
Celebrated
Secured

So if as a researcher you were responsible for tracking down a particular contributor, rather than just putting 'I set up an interview with the architect responsible for the renovations', put 'I secured an interview…' 'Set up' sounds as though all you did was check diaries; secured suggests more of a negotiation and an achievement to get it. Make sure every word on your CV works hard for its keep!

If you were responsible for coming up with story ideas, make it not just 'As part of the team I contributed to weekly ideas sessions', make it 'I developed ideas for the show'.

If you can quantify your successes, be they as an individual or as part of a team effort, it can be a powerful way of reinforcing your success on the programme. So it might be 'Eight of my ideas for segments were filmed' or 'over the course of the series, viewing figures rose to over one million a show.'

> For one corporate I worked for I am able to say 'I led my team to win over £250,000 of new business in our first year.' For one of our clients at Napoleon Creative, I can boast 'that by including the video on the client's site, sales have doubled.'

While you're working on the production, it's really important to record these kinds of statistics. It might be as simple as estimating via Google maps how many miles you covered travelling to four different filming locations or the number of hours of footage generated on a four-day, multi-camera shoot. Adding figures makes your experience seem much more concrete and that you pay attention and engage with the details of the production.

Celebrities

Celebrities are essential to television production. Whether they're a 'I know that face' scientist, a top athlete or a comedian, they can make a show magical to watch and are often pivotal to getting a show commissioned. However, they're not an essential part of your CV. Younger crew in particular seem to fall under their spell, sometimes mentioning more about the celebrity on the programme than they do their role. Celebrities to your average production manager are just another member of the team.

> I remember when I joined one series of a presenter-led programme as a researcher. The first contact I had with him directly was when I took the final script to his dressing room on the studio day. I knocked on his door, he said 'Come in'. I was surprised to find him in just his boxer shorts in the middle of changing into his suit for the recording session. It was a strange moment, meeting someone I'd known from the television for many years and suddenly he's stood in front of me in his underwear. It was like unexpectedly bumping into your boss in the changing rooms of your gym! After a few weeks of encountering him around the office, he soon turned into just another member of the crew.

Unless the programme you're applying for features a celebrity you've worked with, or you worked directly with them within your role on the show, such as directing them or working through scripts with them, only give them a brief mention. Spend the time explaining how good you were at your job!

Awards

If you've worked on productions that have won awards while you were working on them, mention this only if you have a significant role. If you're an edit assistant logging clips or a floor runner for a ground-breaking show, you're not going to have made a significant impact on the show's overall success. Anyone from researcher upwards will have done. If you submit your own films to festivals and get them screened, mention this somewhere too, perhaps in a separate listing section.

> My graduation film was shown at the Telluride Film Festival, at the Filmmakers of Tomorrow section. While there were no awards, one the US newspapers reported it was the 'crowd favourite', so when I listed my film, I put 'considered 'Crowd Favourite' at the Telluride Film Festival. Not a complete lie!

Career Fluctuation

As you look for work in this industry, you sometimes get offered jobs a rung lower than you've been working for previously. I accepted a contract as a researcher when I needed work, although I had previously been working at assistant producer level.

If the roles you've taken are on the same branch of the production tree, for example assistant producer/producer or camera assistant/cameraman, then you have two options here. You can be honest and simply put down the role as you were credited. Everyone knows you go where the work is and we'd rather be working than turning down jobs because they're a grade lower than we'd like.

The alternative is just to list it as the higher of the two roles, since if you've got experience at producer level, you'll still bring the weight of that experience to the position of assistant producer. It is unlikely that the person reading your CV will investigate what the job title was when the credits ran at the end of the show. The most awkward bit would be if they call your referee, and they say 'Actually, she was an assistant producer, not producer'. Hopefully, though, their review will be favourable enough that you'll still come out smelling of roses.

If you're a multi-skilled film maker taking very different roles such as directing, producing and editing, then you'll need to tailor your CV very much according to the advertised role. I cover this later in Chapter 18 - Niche vs Generalist.

Stretching the Truth

On the flip side, you often do the work of the role the next rung up long before getting the screen credit for the role. A little embellishment on your CV can get you through doors which the honest truth would not. I wanted to get a director position and felt I was ready for it as I'd done a little directing while in my researcher roles. I will put my hand up and say I stretched the truth a little and put director on my CV and got the job I was after.

It's a brave move to take; if you talk the talk at the interview, win the job, then on the first day you fail to deliver, you've stained your reputation with that production team. While I fibbed about my job title, I've tried not to lie about my actual skills and level of experience.

Making the Tea

A junior crew member approached Napoleon Creative for work. In his CV, he described his latest job as:

> I was a runner on this production for around two weeks. This involved making tea, looking after cast and crew and buying rigging.

On the previous job to that, he was a runner on another job which:

> involved taking pictures as a location scout and making tea and coffee.

It sounded like he'd learned more about catering than he had about film production. Perhaps the production team didn't want to trust him with anything more complex than boiling a kettle.

We all know that runners often pick up the lousy, menial jobs. Running tapes around the office. Watching dubs dub. Making tea. What did he do with the pictures he took? Did he organise them for the director? Did he create a PowerPoint to show other members of the team? I have no idea.

So for goodness's sake, don't put 'made the tea' on your CV! Tell me about the actual production work you did, the location scouting, what you learned on set. If you only mention your tea-making skills, the only people who will employ you are catering companies.

Chapter 11

Career Breaks

During your career you may well take a career break from television work. It might be because you seized an opportunity to go travelling. If so, I would put a simple line in your CV, making sure you add a comment about how it helped your personal development:

> **August 2005 - February 2006**
> I took time out travelling through Asia before spending three months working in Australia as a surf instructor. It taught me a lot about being self-reliant, I met some amazing people, and improved my teaching skills.

You may start a family and take time out to raise your child. If you're applying for your first job since your maternity leave, I can see that some employers might be concerned that you'll find it complicated going back to full-time work. You might simply not mention at all the reason for your career break within your CV or covering letter. Employing the Inert principle, just state that you took a career break and you're now looking for work again.

If your skills are right for the job, you should get the opportunity to talk with the employer, and see if the reason for your career break comes up. To a certain extent, they have a right to know of any reason why you might not be totally focused on the task in hand, especially if the shoot involves unsociable hours or temporarily relocating to another part of the country. At least if you've got the chance to speak in person, you can explain in more detail about your plans for child care. You certainly should not have to do so at the CV stage.

If you've been back working full-time, and are fitting in childcare quite easily, then I would simply include a line:

January 2008 - March 2009
I took time out to be a full-time Mum.

If you've been working since, it shows that you're perfectly able to juggle a career and childcare.

Another reason for a career break is that you may simply struggle to find work.

In my thirties I relocated to Scotland for a year to work on a series for a regional department of a big broadcaster. I had a great time, and could have continued working there, but London was home.

When the series ended, I headed back to the Big Smoke, my CV piping hot with assistant producer credits. I starting calling around. No interest. I applied for every relevant job. I had a couple of interviews, but no successes. Having worked regionally for two years, I realised my London contacts had gone cold. As this was in the early 2000s, it wasn't easy to stay connected via social networks like LinkedIn and Facebook. I had no inside track for work.

During this time, I took a job with a local council interviewing residents of a large council estate that was due to be demolished. The residents were largely upset that they were being forced to move out of their homes, which some had been living in for forty years. This job had nothing to do with television, but it certainly honed my interview and listening skills.

When I was looking for work, I included this in my CV, after my TV credits, under Non-Creative work (see next chapter). I don't think mentioning this on my CV led to any work directly, but I don't think it did any harm either. Everyone knows this can be a tough career to stay constantly in work, and honesty is the best policy.

Chapter 12

Non-Creative work

As mentioned before, not all your jobs will be within television or the creative fields. Some TV crew have second careers they fall back on. Through my Clearly Creative workshops, I've worked with people who rely on writing, personal training or bar work to keep the wolf from the door.

Think about what you've learned from the non-creative work you've done. Can any of the skills you've picked up be applied to your work in the creative industries? If so, then after your Credits, write a section on 'Non-Creative Work'. Use a similar layout to your TV credits, but keep them brief. You may, though, get to a stage where your Credits list is substantial enough that you choose to not mention this kind of work at all.

If you're new to the industry and need some kind of work experience on your CV, you'll need to list summer jobs and part-time work. Be sparing when mentioning this. As stated earlier, it's better to have a brief one-page CV that shows that you know you don't have much experience than to fill two pages with every detail of your work stacking soft drinks in a supermarket, one of my all-time-dullest jobs.

Concentrate on highlighting the soft skills you learned and the responsibilities you gained. Direct customer service or telephone work is good to list, it shows you have experience of interacting with people. Any control of financial information or handling cash suggest levels of responsibility and trust.

This is an area where once you have a few creative credits to fill the first page-and-a-half of your CV, you can truncate your non-creative experience, giving a series of dates and a summary:

Other Work Experience October 2007 – January 2011
Worked in a range of part-time jobs while at University, including shelf stacking at a local supermarket, bar work and data entry for a pharmaceutical company.

Chapter 13

Training, Software and Education

Now that you've got your Credits out the way, you can list the skills you've learned in 'controlled' environments. For me, training is the list of courses you've done outside formal full-time education. This is often industry-specific training, normally taught part-time or on short courses. They might build additional skills, such as learning another language. Education is formal full-time learning, such as A Levels, Degrees and Masters. Personally, I list Training straight after Credits and then Education since training tends to be more directly relevant to your career than Education.

Training

You should aim to do at least one training course a year, as personal career development. There are plenty of relevant courses you can do that supplement your skills and understanding. This might include learning animation software, Photoshop, GarageBand, a language, or basic acting skills. It's good to spend time in a learning frame of mind and it shows potential employers you have an inquisitive mind and a willingness to learn. It also gives you space to ask stupid questions that you might not want to ask in front of a busy production team. You'll also meet other professionals looking to improve their skills.

When you list the course, it should be:

> **Course** Format, Institution, Date
> What you learned and why it's added to your skills

For me the line about what you got out of the course is important because it shows how what you learned has added another string to your bow.

> **Photoshop** 10-week evening course, City Lit, Autumn 09
> Working with existing assets and my own photographs, this course gave me a better understanding of the key features of Photoshop,

which has improved the way I prepare stills for the edit.

Flower Arranging Weekend course, Birmingham College
A change of pace for me, but helped me develop my eye for composition in a very different creative discipline.

You should also include any Health, Safety and First Aid training you have received. If you've worked for a large company like the BBC it's likely you've done a Health and Safety course. If you haven't, seek one out.

I rate First Aid very highly in staff, especially for filming crew, and it's essential if you're working as an assistant director. As member of a film crew you're put in places which are out of the ordinary, often working with a combination of people you haven't worked with before. While the overall Health and Safety of the crew is the responsibility of the Producer and Production Manager, knowledge of First Aid helps you predict potentially dangerous situations and you have a better idea how to respond if should there be an accident. It also fits with your brand as being a responsible crew member.

So few people mention it on their CV that it is a good way to differentiate yourself from other applicants. For the sake of a hundred pounds and a couple of day's training, you could find yourself able to give confident advice in the event of an accident.

Software

For some roles, particularly editors and animators, you will want to list the software you can operate. I find a simple two or three column list does this effectively without taking up too much room on the page. You should also give an idea of your ability with that package, so:

Final Cut Studio 7 – Advanced
Photoshop CS5 – Confident
After Effects CS5 – Basic

Education

Less-experienced crew sometimes supplement their lack of credits with a list of every single educational qualification they have passed. This is unnecessary and just takes up space that could be left for more important things.

If you've completed a degree or higher, list any qualification post first degree. When listing a university course, be sure to give a flavour of the syllabus, as course titles are often vague. Some studies are purely theoretical, some are practical, so don't just put 'Film and Media Studies,' detail the level of practical work you undertook, what kind of projects and what roles. Mention the number of films you made, or maybe a key one with a significant location or shooting style.

Film Production MA, Northern Media School
I started on the course focusing on Producing and Writing, then went on to direct and edit my own short film as part of my graduation portfolio.

If your degree was more academic, then be sure to explain the subject, and if you wrote an extended piece of written work, such as a dissertation, add what ideas you explored in it.

English and Film Studies BA, Warwick University
This covered a range of English Literature, from Chaucer through to Post-War fiction. Film covered key theoretical and critical approaches to modern cinema. My dissertation explored auteur theory through the works of Tim Burton and Ridley Scott.

If you haven't done a degree, list any qualifications from A Level and above. To be frank, you may have done Film or Media Studies at GCSE, but the harsh reality is that it doesn't really count for much. Sure, you've got an understanding of and have a critical approach to media, but nothing that will really stand you in good stead when you're stepping in to a working environment.

If you didn't complete the course, don't include it on your CV. Again, in an interview situation it can do more damage than good to have to confess to not having finished it.

Languages

List clearly any language skills you have. As with software, a few words to describe your level of ability and whether you know production terms in that language will help Production Managers understand how useful your skills are to their production.

French – Fluent, including production terms
Spanish – Confident

If you're going for a job and you know language skills will be useful and stand as a differentiator, make sure you mention your abilities in both your covering letter and Personal Introduction. Also note my comment about languages in answer-phone greetings, mentioned later in Chapter 22 - The Second Moment of Truth.

Driving

Do mention if you have a driver's licence. If you have experience driving vans or minibuses, that can be useful to add, especially if you're going for production support roles like second or third assistant director.

Don't list any vehicles you own unless they are specifically covered by your insurance company for driving while working.

Chapter 14

Hobbies and Interests

Personal interests are often left off CVs. People feel a bit odd writing them as they're not sure what to put, or why employers would be interested. Well, in our survey, 73% of employers find hobbies and interests relevant to their selection process. They want to know more about you outside of work.

In fact, the most common question I get asked when employers seek a references from me for someone I've employed is 'Do they get on with people?' You can answer this in part before you get to the reference stage by listing some of the things you like to do out of work. Listing your interests gives a little insight into your personality and whether you might fit into the dynamic of the office. Give them something that shows you like interacting with people and what motivates you outside of work. This is a chance to really let your personality come through.

Just like in the Personal Introduction, make sure you don't just put clichés like 'gym, cooking, cinema.' If you're going to write cinema or restaurants, tell them what you like to watch and eat. One workshop participant originally put down 'cooking' but changed this to 'I'm a big fan of Mexican food and have perfected a mean recipe for chilli con carne with lime.' This shows creativity and puts tastes in your mouth as you read it. Don't just put 'Travel,' tell them where you've travelled or would like to travel. Put down a challenging activity you did, like bungee jumping in Australia. It livens up your CV and makes for a more interesting read.

You should always list television or design as one of your hobbies, or else why are you in the industry? I remember my very first interview for the BBC, for a general production role. They asked me what I liked watching on the BBC. Stupidly, I hadn't even given it a thought, and my mind went absolutely blank! Of course, the interviewer wanted to know so she could allocate me to an appropriate programme!

Put down a couple of television shows that you enjoy watching. You need to connect to a broad audience so in your list mention something with popular appeal, not just a niche documentary strand.

Within this section, always list an activity that happens outdoors, away from the office and computer screens.

Chapter 15

References

When I read a CV, I have little way of confirming if what is written down is true. Without doing a bit of digging around, it's hard for me to check that the credit you say you've earned actually rolls up the screen at the end of the TV programme. Even then, if you say you researched and booked the interview, I don't know whether you actually did it, or if you just did the initial searching and then passed it on to an assistant producer to seal the deal.

You need to find a referee whom you trust will confirm that you've achieved what you've claimed to have achieved on your CV. Ideally, you'll choose someone who has more experience and will be a rung or two higher up the production ladder, so they can judge your performance against others doing your job at the same level.

I can't understand why any CV has the words 'Referees available on request'. If you've done the work, been great at what you do, why is there any hesitation about offering up a referee? This is your perfect chance to name drop, show off who you know and who is willing to vouch for you. This is doubly important in the TV industry, where the cross-pollination of staff between productions means that you're not separated by six degrees, it's more like four or even just three. The employer looking at your CV may well have studied or worked with someone connected with a programme you've listed. That kind of personal connection can give your application priority over others. I once got an interview for a job because the production assistant went to university with me. I hadn't seen her since, but I know I got the interview only because of that connection.

One reason applicants give for not listing references is that they don't want an employer being contacted as they're currently working for them. You don't need to worry about this because it's accepted business practice for a potential employer to only approach an applicant's referees once a job offer has been made. Our survey confirmed that 80% of employers will not contact referees until an offer is made. If they know the person stated as a referee, or they know someone who has worked on the same production team as you, 7% will call them up for a discrete chat about you.

Ask people who have employed you to be your referees. You need someone who you feel will talk enthusiastically about you. If you're new to the industry, you should ask one of your tutors at college. You should also ask your referee what method of contact they'd like you to add. You shouldn't put personal contact details down without their permission.

Putting 'on request' achieves nothing, you may as well use the space for other copy. Remember if you're not putting your referees into your CV, you're missing a chance to name drop the people who are prepared to speak for you.

Scratch my back

In all of this activity, remember that you must give as well as receive. Just as you're asking senior members of staff to give you a reference, tell junior members of staff that you're willing to vouch for them. If you hear of a vacancy for which you're either not suitable, or unavailable, then pass it on to a friend or contact. The more you're willing to help other people, the more people will want to help you.

Chapter 16

Branding your CV

In the Clearly Creative survey, we asked employers whether the look and design of the CV was an important factor when they reviewed applications. Three quarters said it was, hardly a surprise in a creative industry. It's an issue of consistency; if you're claiming to have creative talent, your CV needs to reflect this. Times New Roman 12pt isn't going to cut it.

Think about the way you present your CV. The layout. The fonts. The colours you use. You don't necessarily want to make it look like a flyer for a club night in Shoreditch, but a little time and thought spent on the design will show your visual flair and make your CV distinctive and memorable.

Banks, credit card and utilities companies spend millions of pounds researching and consumer testing their documentation to make sure it is legible, it communicates and it gets results. Why not save yourself a fortune and steal branding ideas from the letters that arrive through your door from these companies?

One company that stands out for me is Orange. They have an incredibly clear and distinct brand that seeps through everything they do. No matter what campaign they create, be it ninjas with orange headbands or paper cut-outs, they 'feel' Orange.

If you can achieve in one document what they do across hundreds, of having a unique but crisp look and feel to your document, then you're creating a brand experience when an employer reads your CV.

Take your mobile phone bill. Lay it on the table three feet away. Let your eyes fall on it without trying to comprehend the text. How much space is there? How many logos are there? How easy is it for your eyes to follow where the copy is when you can't read it?

Now pick it up for a closer inspection. Look at the type on the bill. Where do they use different fonts to emphasise different areas of the bill? Where do they use bold? Is the type aligned or justified? Are they using serif or sans serif fonts? Where are the calls to action? These might be other service offerings or requests for payments. Are they highlighted in some way?

Now review two or three other bills. Pick ones that work for you creatively and ones that don't. Sometimes it's easier to see what works when you can compare it with what doesn't.

Now pick up your CV. How does that look in comparison? How does your eye move around the page when it's three feet away? Are the headings clear? Is there enough space? How do the fonts look? How are you guiding the reader's eye to the various parts of the page?

Formatting: The 4 x 2 Rule

Some CVs that I get sent have barely any formatting at all, they're written in Microsoft Word's default font of Times New Roman. Others are overly formatted, with every level of copy a different font size, some italicised, some bold. Visually, it ends up looking busy and hard to read.

Within the Clearly Creative process, I have what I call the 4 x 2 Rule of formatting. There are four variables, which you should have in only two states:

2 x Fonts
2 x Sizes
2 x Weights
2 x Colours

2 x Fonts

You need two fonts, the Primary Font and the Secondary Font. The Primary Font should be used sparingly, and it's usually the more ornate of the two. I don't want to be too prescriptive here, as I want to leave room for you to be creative with your CV, but the Primary Font might be used for your name, then perhaps the different section titles, such as Credits and Education.

The majority of the copy will be in the secondary or body font. This should be a neutral font that is easy to read. There are some key neutral fonts that are available on most computers, like Arial, Verdana, and Times New Roman.

Fonts come in two broad categories, Serif and Sans Serif. Serif fonts have structural extensions at the edges of the letters, such as the curved kick ups at the end of curves of letters like 'C' and the stems of letters like 'L':

Curriculum Vitae

Sans Serif fonts are cleaner, with straight stems:

Curriculum Vitae

Studies have shown that in print, serif fonts are easier to read. However, on screen, the serifs do not show up as well, so since we've already established your CV is most likely to be read on screen, using a sans serif fonts for the body copy is preferable. Personally, I think sans serif fonts work better as body copy as they look crisp and clean. One good rule, though, is to use one of each for increased contrast. If your Primary is serif, have the Secondary sans serif and vice versa.

2 x Sizes

Aside from your name and job role in your Header, you should use no more than two text sizes in your copy, with a substantial difference between the two. Using 12pt and 14pt in the same document does not create enough of a contrast for your eye to easily detect the difference. There should be at least a 30% difference between the two, so 12pt and 16pt. The larger size should be kept for section titles. If you use more than 2 font sizes, although you may feel you're dividing up your CV into different sections, it actually becomes overly complex for the eye to read. Keep it clear and simple.

2 x Weights

Throughout this book I've mentioned using bold to highlight certain sections. When it comes to weights i.e. bold/italicised/underlined etc., I would only use plain text and one other state. I've seen CVs where within one credit listing there's been bold, underline and italics to indicate different kinds of information. This doesn't help, it actually confuses the eye. So keep it simple with just two weights.

2 x Colours

Adding colour can make a distinct difference. Once, I was sat in the office after hours, reading through a stack of CVs looking for crew for a studio shoot that a client had sprung on me at the last minute. I was bored and tired. Then the next one came up and it had a very simple series of green boxes across the top, moving from light green to deep green, a purely decorative embellishment. After acres of black Times New Roman, those little green boxes made me smile. They brightened my life up right then.

I urge you to add a little colour, subtly and sparingly. You might make your name at the top a different colour and if you have certain sections in boxes, make the outlines of the boxes the same shade.

When choosing a colour scheme, think of the inert principle. Bright fluorescent colours are great for drawing attention, but your CV will start looking like a fast food flyer. Keep the colours muted and strictly no more than black copy and one other colour.

Tables

Tables can look very complicated on screen. If you send your CV as a Microsoft Word document, when the reader opens it they'll see not just the table but all the guidelines. If you use tables, my advice is to only use single lines, not double, to outline them and send the document as a PDF so the reader doesn't see the guidelines.

Space

You should make sure there is space in your CV so the first impression is not a bulky mass of copy. This is really important, as there's nothing more disheartening than to open a CV to find a block of text from header to footer. There should be areas of blank space that break up copy and help to let the eye flow down it.

Extreme Makeover

At one of my workshops a participant came with a CV that was adequately laid out in Helvetica. As the group chatted through the session, we found out that she worked as a co-ordinator, setting up stills shoots for a photo library. She set up amazing shoots from women in sexy lingerie to families having holiday fun in the sun, to high shutter speed shots of swimmers. She'd co-ordinated shoots across the world. Her vanilla flavoured CV gave no clue as to her abilities.

When we came to the branding section of the workshop, I suggested that she could put some of the images of the shoots she set up on her CV. I wasn't prepared for the extreme makeover when she sent her new CV for review a few weeks later!

Across the top of the first page she put a light blue strip, on which she put her header information. On the bottom of the page, she put three contrasting images; a woman in a red silk dressing gown reclining (tastefully) on a bed, a dad with his two kids flying down a water flume and a shot of a dusty landscape with a sunset. These images formed a bar the same width as the blue bar at the top. On page two, she put another three images at the top of the page, and a blue bar at the bottom containing her referees' details.

The look of the CV was slick, cool, and contemporary. To be honest, you didn't need to read anything but the header to find out her name and her job title, look at the photos to see the quality of work she'd co-ordinated, then the footer of page two to call her referees! It also showed that she was creative in her own right. In the process of re-writing her CV, she'd added an extra £5,000 to her perceived annual salary. That's enough to buy a top spec MacBook Pro, the latest Adobe Creative Suite and Final Cut Pro, a HD handycam and still have change for a weekend in Paris to go filming! Shortly after rebranding her CV, she won a new contract with another agency.

If you're in a creative role like an animator, camera person, director or art designer, your CV can become a portfolio in itself. A few carefully selected shots will entice the reader to check out your showreel. Check out the range of CVs at CVParade.com for some of the most creative around. The trick, though, is balancing the 'content' with the 'design'. You don't want to have so much decoration that you neglect to communicate your work experience and skills.

Chapter 17

Version Control

If you've followed the Clearly Creative process to this stage, you should have a master CV. This might spread on to three or four pages, with every bit of work experience you've ever had. Your next challenge will be to condense this CV to fit the two page limit discussed earlier.

This challenge is one of organisation, keeping track of multiple versions of your CV on your computer. Set aside a folder on your computer or cloud storage solely for your CV (www.dropbox.com is a great tool that lets you store docs on multiple devices). Before we chat about reversioning, a word or two about naming files. You wouldn't believe the number of people who deliver their CV in a file called CV.doc. That's really stupid. How is your CV possibly going to stand out if your potential new employer has saved all the files into one folder to view? If they've read your CV and put your name on the shortlist, how are they going to find your CV quickly and easily on the day of the interview?

My absolute favourite CV name was labelled 'CV - Accurate.' I'm so pleased they didn't send me the one they've called 'CV - Completely Made Up' though I probably would have read it with great interest!

Your CV should be labelled with your name, perhaps your role, and with some kind of date indicator:

Robin_Smith_Editor_CV_April_2012.doc

Giving your CV a title like this looks organised, which show consistency because your CV is too. Adding the date is a neat trick as the April version need be no different than the January one, save the date stamp, but it seems like it's your freshest, most up-to-date CV. It makes you appear current, methodical and that as well as being creative you can be accurate and organised.

So in this vein, save the master file you've created with an appropriate name. For example, you might call it YourName_Master_CV.doc. That way you're clear which is your original kitchen sink version.

Proofing

Once you've written your master CV, set it to one side. Leave it for a day, or preferably two, then print it out and read it afresh. I suggest printing it out because when you're reading it again and again on your screen using the same computer programme, you can become blind to the copy. Printing it out delivers the document to you on a completely different medium, and you are more likely to spot mistakes. Another trick is to read it out loud. The action of reading the words will engage your brain in a different way and again, you'll highlight mistakes you don't see when just reading.

Be careful of grammar and spelling. Don't be caught out by homonyms: words that sound the same but have different spellings and meanings. You need to know the difference between special effects and special affects. Practice is not the same as practise; one is a verb, the other is a noun. You also need to know the distinction between their, there and they're. Watch out for apostrophes and contractions. I'm not going to get into a lesson in grammar and spelling here, there are plenty of books dedicated to this that can do a much better job. What you need to know is that sloppy English will lose you points with your potential new employer.

You should also at this stage get a friend or relative to read it for you. Let them give you feedback not just of grammatical and spelling mistakes, but also understanding. If they know about the television industry, get them to describe what they think you do from what you've written. This will help you see where there are gaps between what you think you're communicating and what people are drawing from your writing.

Editing

Now go through your master and streamline the content to fit on just two sides. Your earlier career needs less explanation that your latest jobs. If you have a longer work history, you might truncate your credits. For example, if you're now a producer, you might just put:

Researcher, Various Production Companies, 2001-2004
I worked as a researcher for two years on a variety of productions, including chat shows and antiques programmes. More details on request.

Save this version with an appropriate title. Then compare it with your master. Have you really lost anything? Hopefully not.

Bespoke CV

Whichever CV you end up sending, be sure to tailor it according to the job advertised. You might want to change the projects you mention in your Personal Introduction, so that they match closely the job for which you're applying for. You might add a little more copy on your most relevant projects and cut others down or completely out. Keeping your Master CV to hand, it should be easy to cut and paste together a perfectly tailored document that will reflect the skills required by the job description.

Format

Your employer is most likely to be reading on screen, so if you send your CV as a Word doc, all your spelling mistakes will be underlined in red! I would advise delivering as a PDF, a standard document format. This enables the CV to be seen as an image, rather than editable text. If you have used tables to format your text, you'll only see any lines you've added, not the guidelines. The PDF format also enables you to easily add hyperlinks to your email address and websites. This means that in one click your potential employer can create a new email addressed to you without having to worry that they might not get your email address right. They're also more likely to visit your show reel if all they have to do is click rather than typing out the URL. If you really want to be useful, on each programme listing you can add links to the micro sites for the programme on the broadcaster's website or to clips of the programme on your site or YouTube.

There are various routes to make a PDF from a word processor document, Google is your friend to find the best one according to the software package and operating system you're working on.

The one downside of PDFs is that they're not always very good at translating non-standard fonts into graphics, sometimes substituting them for standard fonts. You'll need to spend some time previewing how your CV looks before sending it. The alternative is to use a graphics software package like PhotoShop to create your name or headings in the desired photo and colours, saving them as individual images in jpg/png/giff format, then inserting these into Word. When the PDF is generated, it will embed these images into the PDF.

Be warned, creating a graphics heavy PDF from a Word document is an arcane science; unless you know what you're doing it can be a fiddly job. This is not something to start when you only have an hour to complete your CV and post it!

Chapter 18

Niche vs Generalist

Working in television production, you'll develop a wide range of skills and knowledge according to the genre, format, target audience and budget level of the programme you work on. Over the years, almost certainly you'll gravitate towards a particular type of programme on which you work most often, whether intentionally or not. This can work in your favour, since your CV is so strong in one particular area that you're sought after for your expertise. When you apply for similar jobs, you can use your CV to play to this strength as employers like to hire people who've already been employed in a job similar to the one they're crewing.

> When my company was pitching to a technology company that was looking for a film to show their high-tech workshop. We showed them our latest work, a short documentary following the renovation of a large Victorian school as it was brought up to modern building, environmental and disabled access standards. Unknown to us, the tech company owners were involved in a similar redevelopment. They loved the film, and we won not only the commission we pitched for, but another to make a video about their redevelopment project. They effectively bought exactly the same project we'd already made.

Niche experience can also be a weakness. It can be tough moving between programme types when you get pigeonholed into one area or one specific role. You get rejected for not having the experience that matches the conditions of the job, even if your skills were entirely transferable.

> When choosing between two camera people, I turned down someone because they didn't have experience of working on conferences and the other did. When I spoke to the camera man to turn him down, he told me that I'll always get what I've always had if I don't try someone who might look at the

situation differently. Yes, I absolutely agree and actually, I try whenever possible to bring fresh talent to my teams, people whose work is different to what we've done, so we get new ideas thrown into our creative mix. For this particular job, however, it was a high pressure conference and it was more important to hire someone who had experienced that environment before taking a chance on someone I'd not worked with before who hadn't.

When writing versions of your CV, you can create one that focuses on your niche and one that is generalist, to open up the widest opportunities.

Niche

If you want your CV to play to your strengths, you need to start by identifying your niche, which is most often your specialist area of knowledge or a particular filming technique. It might be working with children, a knack for observational documentary filming technique, or a knowledge of a particular area of science. This is where you're communicating the depth of your skills.

When I worked for the BBC on Film 99, I had daily contact with film distributors, PR companies and agents. That job led to research work on documentaries about films stars, like Hollywood Greats, made by the same department. When I started to look for work, I highlighted the skills I had in this area. My knowledge of copyright, of working with US-based film distributors to license footage and my contacts at UK film distributors and PR companies. This meant that when I applied for jobs working on programmes about films or ones with archive footage requirements, I usually got to the interview stage. I didn't win all of those jobs by any means, but I got short listed because I'd shown I was a specialist.

You can tailor your CV to highlight your niche skills, so when an appropriate job comes up you're a perfect fit.

Generalist

On the other hand, you'll also see and want to apply for jobs that are very different in format or subject. You'll almost certainly have the right skills, just gained on different programmes that you can transfer to the new position. For these kinds of jobs you can create a generic CV that dilutes the niche nature of your work history.

> In my case, rather than writing 'regular contact with film PR companies' I just wrote 'PR companies'. By missing out film as the theme, I made my experience sound broader. When talking about the show, I focused on the format - a magazine show - rather than the content. I talked about filming at live events, instead of film premieres, interviewing guest celebrities not film stars. This made my skills sound more relevant to any other magazine show, rather than exclusively for film shows, and therefore more transferable.

Role Specific CVs

Technology has progressed so much in the last ten years that everything you need to create a TV programme can be carried in two small rucksacks, one with a HD camera, the other with a laptop. With this innovation has come new multi-role positions, such as the self-shooting producer/director. They film footage themselves, watch budgets while they're filming in the field, then cut their own material.

Producers don't always want a multi-role technician, they want someone with specific skills. When I'm looking to recruit an editor, I want someone who sits hunched over an edit suite day in, day out, as they will have a much deeper understanding of the editing software, short cuts and styles than a producer/director who only edits part time.

If you're multi-skilled, you might need a different CV for each key role that you're capable of performing. Make sure that you put the specific role beneath your name at the top in the Header. Clear your mind of your other duties you performed on the production and zero in on the skills you need to win that specific job.

Imagine you are a self-shooting Producer/Director, who is going after a job as an editor. Instead of writing your job descriptions detailing the filming side to your duties, tell them a story about the editing you did, what platform you cut it on, whether you delivered the final piece for broadcast. This will give the reader more confidence in your role-specific skills.

Chapter 19

Ready to Go

Once you have these various CVs in your folder, you're ready to go. If you've followed these tips, you've achieved getting your CV to be Clearly Creative.

Your header will stand out, with your role clearly defined.

You'll have given your contact details clearly, as well as provided links to easily access your showreel and online profiles.

You'll have a simple, factual personal statement that will communicate the breadth and depth of your experience without resorting to sensational adjectives.

The list of job titles you've had will be optimised for scanning, so your climb up the career ladder is clear at a glance.

Job Credits will explain something about the programmes listed to those who've not seen an episode, as well as detailing what you did while working on them.

Your Training and Education will mention not just the courses taken but what you learned from them.

You'll have revealed a little personal detail by sharing your hobbies and interests.

And you'll have finished this off with a list of referees who will speak up for you and confirm that what you've put in your CV is correct.

Now you have to think about how you're going to deliver your brand, spanking-new CV.

PART 3: Delivery

Chapter 20

Applying

When a job opportunity is brought to your attention, if you're like me, your instinct tells you to apply quickly because many online ads disappear once the advertiser has been swamped with applicants.

> I remember reading a job listing when I was a freelancer director and in the time it took me to write my application on ProductionBase, it was taken down. I desperately called the production company because I had the relevant experience and wanted to get my CV under the employer's nose. After charming the receptionist, I managed to leave a voice mail on an assistant's phone asking for the email address of the production manager so I could send in my CV. Needless to say, I never got a call back so I couldn't make an application. I didn't even get considered for the job, even though I knew I could do it, simply because I was a minute or two late.
>
> I've also been on the other side of the interview table, suspending a job ad after an hour because forty people had applied for the role; I was under pressure to get the crew for the shoot confirmed and from a quick scan of the applications I was confident that at least three or four of the applicants could handle the job and I didn't have time or the need to look through any more.

As part of our survey, we asked a range of employers: do you read CVs as they come in or wait and stock pile them to read all together? The results came back pretty much fifty-fifty. Half of them read them straight away, which means they're reading your CV in the middle of other tasks at work. The other half are reading them having just read another candidate's, and will follow yours with yet another.

The thing to learn here is that you don't know if being first to apply will mean your CV is read earlier or whether it will fall to the bottom of someone's in-tray. What you have to make sure is that you spend enough time getting the covering note right, as this will have a greater impact than being the first applicant to drop through the electronic letter box.

The key is being as prepared as possible. Your CV and covering letter need to be on hand and ready at all times, so that you can spend a little time customising them before sending them promptly.

Paper Applications

If you're sending on paper, make sure the quality of stationery is decent. It doesn't need to be parchment paper, but better than standard photocopying paper. Use an envelope from the same range to ensure you're presenting a consistent look. Personally, I favour a good, crisp, neutral white rather than cream. If you've got time and legible handwriting, I'd advise handwriting any correspondence that goes with the CV. Very few people receive post, and even fewer handwritten letters, so it may well stand out and snatch you an extra thirty seconds of attention over the other post to be read that day.

Within the envelope you should consider including a business card and a postcard. With the likes of Moo.com, it's very cheap to get good quality, personalised stationery printed. Print costs for small-run printing has plummeted in recent years. A set of business cards and some postcards won't even set you back £50. Pick a few stills from your work and put them together to create a postcard. Again, I'd avoid putting a photo of yourself on the card.

Keep the design consistent with the branding you've chosen for your CV, copying the fonts, weights, sizes and colours from the 4 x 2 rule. If design software isn't your strong point, look in your network for someone to help. Offer to pay back the favour in some way, exchanging an hour or two of their Illustrator skills for an hour or two reading their CV or cutting together some of their images to music for their website. Failing that, you can always use services like elancer.com or 99designs.co.uk, crowd sourcing to find people to do the design work for you at a low cost.

Your objective with the postcard is to make something that people will want to stick somewhere near their desk because it looks nice. Make sure you put your contact details on the back, but leave the majority of it blank to keep them versatile: you can use them as thank you cards, compliment slips or for sending simple messages. Then hopefully, the card will keep catching their eye until eventually they pick it up and call you!

Gimmicks

I've heard many stories of unusual CVs. At one point, tea bags were the cool thing to include, with a note cheerfully saying 'have a cup of tea on me while you read my CV.' That one's been done to death.

My favourite was told to me by a friend who works in a central London post-production house. A CV arrived in a big manila folder covered in stars and glitter, which spilled all over her desk. This was accompanied by the applicant's original exam certificates including sporting achievements. The person was swiftly contacted and politely asked to collect their certificates before they were filed in the bin. Needless to say this didn't make a good impression! Avoid gimmicks at all cost.

Chapter 21

Covering Letter

Your covering letter is the first contact you have with your potential employer, whether it's the note you put in the envelope with your CV when sent by post, the body copy of the email to which your CV is attached, or the form you complete online to submit your profile for consideration. This first contact is another opportunity to stand out from the crowd so it's vital you get it right. So, why do cover letters fail?

Too Formal

Emails often start with 'Dear Sir or Madam' or 'To Whom It May Concern'. This is followed by a very stoically written paragraph on why that person is brilliant at what they do. These notes can be entirely devoid of anything that actually warms me to them; I want to read something that is polite but friendly and engaging.

Information Repeated

Some covering letters fail because they give information about the applicant's work history already there in the CV. There's no point simply repeating content.

The Goldilocks Length

The most annoying of all are those that simply say 'Please find attached my CV for consideration.' This is a wasted opportunity. Then there are those applications that really take a long time saying nothing at all. Here's one I received:

> I have a lot of media experience that I'd like to put to good use. I hope you find my background interesting. Let me tell you a little bit about myself...where should I start? I slipped into TV production by chance. This was the early 90s and I rose quickly in the ranks, doubled my salary in two years and had my own show running on one of the largest commercial stations with an average of 46% of the target group tuning in every week.

To be honest, if I wasn't so interested in helping people improve the way they look for work, I'd have stopped reading at 'my background interesting' and deleted the email. Even then, I only got as far as the excerpt above. I still have no idea what this person does for a living, and to be honest, I don't have time to find out. Neither does the production manager who gets these kinds of emails all the time. They'll simply delete it.

Direct and to the point

If you're going to send an email looking for work, then make it quick and painless. Try something along these lines:

> I am a [role] and you can see my current showreel here [hyperlink to your showreel]. I've attached my CV for more details. My main experience is with…

Then start telling me what you do. And when you do, I want you to charm me.

Flirting

I think most people look at the covering letter as a broadcast. A statement. A declaration of intent to win the job. It's not.

The covering letter is where you open your dialogue with your potential new employers, it's your first conversation with them. You're hoping they'll respond to you positively.

To help you get into the right frame of mind, imagine you've been invited by a fellow filmmaker to a wrap party for a short she's just produced. You don't know many people there, but everyone is having a good time. It's the kind of party where everyone's dressed up nicely, with cast, crew and their guests mixing together.

Your friend sees someone across the room she hasn't seen for a year, and heads over to say hello, leaving you to entertain yourself. You feel a bit of a lemon. The person standing near you also looks by themself. They're a little older than you. Perhaps you could strike up a conversation with them. How would you approach them?

Well, a good start would be a friendly hello. You'd introduce yourself with your first name. In this situation, I find myself giving my relationship to the party context, explaining how I'm connected to the hosts, a simple 'I'm friends with Robin, we studied at University together.'

This is exactly the frame of mind you need when writing your covering letter. Start with Hello or Hi rather than Dear and use their first names, if you can find out the name of the person to whom you're applying, though this can be increasingly difficult. Next you need to give context to your email or letter, to be clear about why you're writing to them. Mention the specific role you're applying for and how you heard about it or saw it advertised. There's a practical reason for this. When crewing up a television programme, several positions are often advertised at once, so you need to make it easy for them to know which role you're hoping to fill as different people may be involved in the selection of each role. It's useful for them to find out how you heard about the position as they might be using multiple ads, so this way they'll find out which is the most effective.

Now, back at the party, imagine you quite fancy the person you're chatting to. You'd like to get to know them better. How would you do this? Probably a good place to start would be by paying them a compliment. Say something nice about their watch, their clothes, their tattoo. A gentle comment that's not too forward, but shows that you've noticed them on that level. Something that gives them chance to flirt a little back if they're mutually interested.

Within your covering letter, pay a compliment to the producer or production manager to whom you're writing. Just like the party guest, a positive comment is going to warm them to you. It's going to give you something in common (unless the tattoo was the result of a tequila-fuelled dare back at college). It's inviting them to talk about themselves, even if this is just in their heads as they read your letter. In a social situation, no one likes the party bore who only talks about themselves. So why would you only write about yourself in your covering letter? Yet this is what so many people do.

In the Clearly Creative survey, employers said only 30% of applicants name-checked the company offering the work in their covering letter. That means that if you simply say 'I like Napoleon Creative's work' then straight away you stand out.

I wanted to dig a little deeper into this phenomena, so I looked at the applications we had for all the jobs we advertised during the previous year. Out of 212 applications, only 22% mentioned our company by name. Think about it. You're applying for a specific job, you need to at the very least name-check the company in your letter.

Better still, you need to show you're interested in working for them by telling them you like about their projects. Yet out of those 212 applications, only 3% actually made any reference to our work. How rude is that? Imagine you're at a badly run speed dating event. You meet thirty people. Only one actually gives you space to talk about yourself, rather than them. Who, out of the thirty eager romantics, is going to stand out?

Find one or two projects on the company's showreel that you genuinely find interesting or entertaining and compliment them. You should also explain the reason why to give your compliment a substance. Flatter them. As an employer, it always makes me look at that person's CV far more fully, since they're shown an interest in my work. Remember, the covering letter is not a monologue, its the opening line to a dialogue.

When we posted a job ad for a presenter for a job we were doing, one presenter's application stood out a mile because he said this:

> I loved your website. What an impressive client list! I particularly liked your film about the Motasem wedding dress collection. Very stylish and atmospheric.

Covering letters are usually all about the applicant saying why they'd be great for the role, not about why they want to work for us. The fact that he'd researched us and showed an interest in us made me spend a good amount of time on his CV and showreel. Unfortunately, he wasn't quite right for the job we had in hand, but when the right job does come up, I'd like to work with him. I connected with him on Twitter and LinkedIn so he can stay on my radar. He might not have got the job he applied for, but he will go far if he keeps making that kind of positive impression when he applies for work.

The other advantage of giving compliments, apart from the direct flattery, is that you come across as a positive person. Someone who is able to look on the brighter side of life. Someone who creates an atmosphere that's a pleasure to be around. That's the kind of person you want to have on your team when you're stood in a field in the Isle of Wight on a bitter winter morning to film the sun coming up over the horizon. It contributes to the way people engage with you emotionally, one of the factors that sways purchasers.

Getting down to business

We've covered all the soft, fluffy stuff, now you need to get down to business and make your claim on that job. At Napoleon Creative, we reviewed our pitching process and realised that we weren't being clear enough when stating how our ideas matched what was being asked for in the project brief. Now at the beginning of every proposal we clearly state 'We understand that you are looking for…' This wasn't the only change we made during this review, but we have noticed a much better response from our pitches.

We don't always interpret the client's needs perfectly; we're unlikely to get it spot on until we've spoken to the client in more detail. However, it is a very powerful statement that makes them feel that we have listened to their brief (be it during a phone conversation or in a formal tender document) and we're trying to anticipate their needs. You can use the same technique by considering the role advertised and the specific skills called for, and then explaining how you're perfect for that role. You might try something like:

> I understand that you're looking for a cameraman with observation documentary experience. I worked on an OB Doc for a year working in hospital…

> You're searching for a researcher for your programme about 70s design, so you'll need someone with an extensive knowledge of art history and domestic interiors. While at University I studied Architecture…

You might not hit the nail on the head for the person reading the CV, but it will show you are thinking about solutions. You are not just responding to an ad, you're looking at how you can solve their headaches for them. 'Phew,' they'll think,'you have an attitude of self-sufficiency, I'm not going to have to babysit you through the production, you're able to think for yourself.'

Find Out More

Sometimes you know very little about the job, and I think this is very much the fault of the employers. They post an ad with a sparse description, then wonder why they're inundated with inappropriate responses. If employers gave more details of the programme, they'd get more targeted applications. So how do you get around this? Well, here's where you need to be really crafty.

First, don't go directly to the production company if you can avoid it. See if you can find someone in your contacts who can help. This is where LinkedIn can be very helpful as you can search for people you know who've worked with the company in question. See if you can reach out to find out more information about the vacancy without direct contact.

Failing that, give the production company a call. Now, this takes a really specific strategy. When we post jobs, usually we do it through a jobs website that requires a subscription fee, such as ProductionBase. Paid-for sites deliver a better quality of applicant. The applications are in a standard format that makes it easier for us to manage the selection process. However, we usually get a few calls to the office, even if we specify 'No calls to the office'. Often people want to know how to apply directly, as they don't subscribe to the job website. How I respond to this will depend on my mood and the number of applicants. If I've already had twenty emails, I might insist they apply through the website. Often I'll just ask them to email me direct, after all they've made the effort to pick up the phone and show interest.

The question I hate to be asked is 'Can you tell me more about the project?'. This question hangs in the air like a bad smell. I hate answering it. I make a point of explaining the key elements of the shoot in the ad. The open-ended nature of the question makes me react with a simple 'I don't have time.' My day is too busy to take time out to tell everyone who phones up the details of the job. Plus, why should they get additional information, advantageous to their application, not passed on to the others who have followed our 'No calls to the office' instruction?

How about instead, you enquire 'Can you just tell me the format of the project so I can check I've got the right skills for the job before applying?'. This is a completely different question. It's straightforward. It can be answered in two or three words. There's no sense of discussion and the person asking is trying to work out whether to waste my time or not, and if I spend ten seconds answering, I'm spared reading their CV if they've only done studio programmes and this is outside broadcast work.

Relevance

While production skills are often transferable, there are some cases where the ad mentions specific skills or requirements. If you don't fit them, or can't stretch your CV to fit, then don't apply.

We posted an ad for local crew for a job in Norwich. We target local crew when filming outside of London for several reasons. If they live locally, you pay less travel expenses. Also, they're starting their day with twenty minutes travel time instead of three hours, which means they'll have more energy for filming, while I (who will have got up at 6.00am to be there at 9.00am) will be falling asleep. Most importantly, they have local knowledge, so if a bit of kit breaks, they'll know where we can get a replacement, and, most importantly, they'll know a good pub for lunch.

I also believe that as there are far fewer opportunities outside of London for film and television you should give local crew consideration before exporting people from London.

When we looked through the applicants, we got very few from people who lived actually in Norwich or the surrounding area. There's not a huge amount of media work there, so we knew we weren't going to be inundated with replies. We got a few who had family in Norfolk, and were happy to cover the travelling themselves. Fair enough, though I don't like this, because essentially you're paying for your own transport which should be covered by production. The point here, however, is they made a relevant application.

One applicant sent us this:

> Multi skilled camera operator - That's me! Wow, I've had a look at the ad, it suits me down to a tee! My greatest passion in the world is working with moving pictures being a visual storyteller. I love working in a team dealing with a lot of different interviewees and cases. Being able to do it in a vibrant and exciting place like ITN, is a dream for me. I've heard only positive things about ITN from freelancers who are working with you.

And so it went on. And on. And on. Over 500 words of cut'n'paste drivel and at the end? An address in Chiswick. Which isn't even in East London, let alone East Anglia.

Clearly, this applicant has just seen an ad for a camera person, and hit apply. I think they simply copied a previous application (hence the references to ITN) as they hadn't read or responded to the details of the ad itself. What does this say to me? The camera person is so desperate they'll reply to any position in the hope of getting work. This kind of scatter gun approach to applying for everything is really annoying to an employer.

Target your applications, target your copy. Make your covering letter friendly, complimentary, and respond clearly to the criteria listed in the vacancy, or it will turn your potential employee off even if your skills are a match made in heaven.

State Your Rate

Whenever I advertise a job, I ask freelancers to give their rate. Sometimes this is because I also need camera kit, and I'd rather give the camera person an extra fee to hire their camera than get it in from a production house. If it's their own, then they'll know the kit inside out and how to get the most out of it. And of course, if I ask for a rate, I might get lower offers than I had budgeted for. So few people reply with a rate. I find it incredibly frustrating and often wonder why they people don't want to tell me what they'd like to get paid.

Picture a high stakes game of poker, set in a high class casino, a setting worthy of a James Bond novel. In your hand, you hold a low flush. You're confident you can win this. There's £1,200 left in your wallet, your week's wages. Your new employer is sat opposite, and they're looking a little nervous. You can bluff your way through this, just keep your cool, and whatever you do, don't show your hand yet....

Actually, it's not like that at all. Now step inside a dusty local stationery shop. The kind where they sell everything, even fax machine rolls (Google if you're too young know what these are) but the service is slow and they're a bit hopeless. However, the shop is right next door to the production office and you need a clipboard for a last-minute shoot. They have seven different clipboards available, but only four have prices. Can you really be bothered to pick up an unpriced one, find a shop assistant, ask how much it is? You know that if you take it to the till, they'll only have to look it up in one of the fourteen stock books under the counter. Really, it's just a clip board, grab the priced one you like the most and take it to the till. It's not worth more of your time.

If you're asked for a rate, give it. Don't put up obstacles. You should know what you day rate is, pitched according to your level of skill and experience. When quoting for each job, be sure to take into account what the job requires. If it's completely below your experience level but you'd rather be working than not, discount your price down, saying 'My usual rate is £350 but I'm happy to do this for £250.' If it's a short or half day, again, drop your rate. It shows flexibility. Start a dialogue where you're happy to be flexible with rates, because sometimes budgets are tight, and some jobs are easier than others, and being willing to show flexibility will make you firm friends with every production manager.

Don't, however, take it as far as one camera person did. I advertised a one day job, and by the time I reached forty applications I pulled the ad. When you apply through ProductionBase, you can actually see how many other people have applied. One inexperienced guy wrote 'Due to the high number of applications you've had already, I'll drop my daily rate to just £75!'

This makes me hang my head. Just because you're in competition, don't drop your rates so far you're not making any money at all. It's not going to look favourably on you. You're doing yourself down. Of course, you're always going to need to negotiate on price, because everyone's being squeezed, as a production company our clients are always pressurising us to reduce costs. Just don't cut your rate before you've even heard the starting gun!

It's worth trying to win every job, because it's not just about that individual job. One cameraman I employed for a one day job four years ago now does a great deal of our camera work. In that time I've taken him to China, Vietnam and the Philippines filming. He's put his rate up by 30% and I'm still happy paying his invoices. Just like the way supermarkets discount new products so you're tempted to try them out, with the hope you'll buy them again when they're full price, use short one off jobs as routes in to working with new companies who will hopefully call you directly for the next one.

Build a library

Covering letters, like your CV, will become very formulaic. Whenever you apply for a job, be sure to save the covering letter as a document on your computer. In the file name, add keywords that will help you remember on what skills and experiences you focused. It might be 'BBC self shooting' or 'ITV film research skills'.

If you get an interview, you can easily review what it is you told them. Second, you'll build a library of responses so that when you need to write a covering letter, you can copy and paste from other applications, then bespoke it for the particular application. This will enable you to respond to job ads promptly and with little hassle.

If you respond to ads from your mobile phone, you might want to find a way of storing a few key covering letters on it, so you can cut and paste the most appropriate into a fresh email, bespoke it then send.

Signature

When you start your dialogue with your potential new employer, one easy trick to miss is adding an automated signature to every email. I've been in situations where I've engaged in email conversations with a freelancer, and after three or four emails, checking availability and rates, I want to call them. I can't find their number. The email with their CV is buried deep in my inbox, or maybe I only saw it on their CV online on ProductionBase. Do I really want to log back in, find their profile and look for their number? No, I want them to include it on each email.

This is easy to set up, either in the settings of your email software package or on your email provider's website. Basically, it should have the same information as your header:

Name
Role
Contact number
Website

So mine reads:

Gavin Ricketts
Founder/Creative/Agitator

020 7871 7768
www.napoleoncreative.com

If I do have to scour my inbox for an applicant's number, it'll take me time. In the meantime, another application might take my eye.

Reduce Response Time

There's a theme through all of this activity. It's all about reducing response time. You need to minimise the time it takes for an employer to warm to your application and take action.

Through applying the Clearly Creative process to writing your CV, you've reduced the time it takes for them to understand your skills and assess your suitability to the job.

Archiving your covering letters so that you can open one up, bespoke it and send reduces the time between discovering the opportunity and making your application.

Having your contact details available clearly at every point of contact reduces the time between your new employer making the mental decision that you're an appropriate candidate to contact and the actual physical act of picking up the phone and dialling your number. Believe it or not, the chasm between these two events can be hard to bridge! In between the decision and the action, another phone call might come in, perhaps from a freelancer they've worked with before and maybe they'll simply employ them instead.

By reducing response time at each stage, there's less time for your competitors to get in there with their applications and the recruiter will have a smoother, easier experience in getting to the Second Moment of Truth; when they pick up the phone and call you.

Chapter 22

The Second Moment of Truth

As an employer, once I've gone through all the CVs I reach a point where I've narrowed the stack of applications to maybe five. It's time for me to pick up the phone. If the CV and covering letter is the First Moment of Truth I have with a crew member, then the phone call is the Second.

I don't expect freelancers to answer their mobiles first time. They might be working on a shoot where they can't take calls. I do despair, though, when I call the number and I get greeted by the woman I affectionately call Autobot Lady, the automated answer-phone system. Have I called the right number, or did I misdial? Shall I leave a message? Quite often I will simply hang up and move on to the next applicant. I'm not the only one who does this.

In our Clearly Creative survey we asked people responsible for employing crew like you: 'What do you do when you call a freelancer for the first time and get an automated answer-phone message?'

Here are the startling results. Of the respondents, 66% will leave you a message. Of those, a third will have a bad impression of you if they are greeted by an automated answer-phone message. A further 13% will hang up without leaving a message and will call back later. In the meantime, however, they may well have got through to other applicants and have filled the interview slots or even the job before they get around to it! The most important statistic is this:

20% will NOT call back.

So, you've made it through the cull of perhaps 90% of the applications, but if you haven't got a voice mail message, you've lost out on one in five jobs. This astounded me, but I know it's true.

At one of my workshops, I was telling the group about the importance of the voicemail message. Several attendees were skeptical. Then a production manager in the group admitted, yes, she doesn't leave a message to an Autobot. I asked her if she had a voicemail message, she confessed she didn't know. I put my mobile on speakerphone and called her number. When it clicked through to the voicemail Autobot Lady answered. She was very embarrassed when she discovered that she hadn't implemented something so simple that influenced her own selection of candidates!

Personalised Message

Recording your own voicemail message is a chance to show you have a clear, understandable telephone voice. By having a warm, welcoming tone, you again reinforce, like the compliments on your covering letter, that you're a positive person to be around, another emotional connection point.

If you do have another language, you could always leave your message twice, once in English then in the other language. This will demonstrate to the person calling that you have another language, something they might have missed from your CV.

If English is not your first language, it can also help to put an employer's mind at rest about the standard of your spoken English.

If you're really clever, you'll change your voicemail message every day, making it specific to that day's activities. This is particularly effective for crew who spend most of their days on set:

> "Hi, it's Tuesday the 4th, I can't take your call because I'm in Park Royal filming a car commercial. Please leave a message after the tone."
>
> "Hello, sorry I can't take your call, I'm body painting all day for a kid's TV show. Leave a message and I'll call you back."

How cool does that sound to your potential employer? Remember, though, this only works if you dot from job to job, and you remember to update your message regularly. If your employer calls in March to find out you're still art directing Santa's Grotto, your skills won't sound in great demand.

Recording

If you're not confident at leaving a message, write out what you're going to say and rehearse it. When it comes to recording the message, make sure you're in a quiet room. Take a deep breath as Autobot Lady is starting to cue you in, so once the beep goes, you can confidently breathe out and start your message. Otherwise the first thing the person hears is your sharp intake of breath!

If you don't like what you've recorded, try again until you get something that sounds warm, calm and inviting.

Chapter 23

Following Up

If a new employer contacts you, either by email or phone, you've done well. They've picked you out from many applicants to be seriously considered for the role. To be honest, it means you can almost certainly do the role, as can all the others selected at this stage. Then it's a question of which candidate performs best in the interview, which one has experiences that resonate strongest with the project or who will seem the best fit with the production team.

If you don't get any further, remember it's like the Oscars. It's not just the winner who gets the kudos, it's all the nominees. If you've been selected for interview, but not secured the job, do not forget that you have won a new contact. Someone who has shown interest in you. They might have been impressed by your work, you just might not be quite right for the particular role. Having made that connection, you mustn't let it go.

Ask for the Work

If you've been interviewed or received a phone call, then you've obviously ticked enough of their 'need' criteria. Be sure to get their name and contact details when they call. If you don't hear from them after a couple of days, call them. I often surprised by how few people follow up and ask for the work.

> We had a project to be delivered on DVD. We did a ring around of three key players in the duplication business to see who had the best deal. The project was delayed, so we didn't pursue the quotes we were sent after the initial contact. Only one firm actually followed up their quote with a phone call. In fact over the next few months they called a couple of times, always polite, always happy to take no for an answer. They asked if we were happy with the quote, we said some of the other quotes had been slightly cheaper. They said they could work something out. Six month later, we finally had the project finished and

ready for duplication. We couldn't even remember the names of the other firms we originally spoke to, only the one who called back. Guess who won our business?

Polite persistence can work wonders. Picking up the phone and reiterating that you're keen to work with them. Showing understanding of any delays. Again, it's building a relationship and trust with them. If a decision hasn't been made, you could even brazenly ask what would swing the work your way?

Income-Generating Activity

At one sales training seminar as part of the on-going development of my production company, I was advised that as a business owner I should be doing between an hour and three hours of income-generating activity every day. That's not the work that you get paid to do, that's the work you do to make sure you win work to get paid for. In the case of a TV freelancer, it's not the work done editing, producing or directing, it's the work done to make sure you have a project to work on, the internet searches, phone calls and emailing.

As a TV crew member, you're really, really lucky if you finish one job on the Friday and start the next on the Monday. Usually, there's a week, maybe two between each contract. Over the year, you'll spend, say eight weeks not working. Statutory holiday entitlement in the UK is 5.6 weeks. That means you have 2.4 weeks not working but not on holiday either. This time needs to be spent working on your career. Going on training courses, writing up your CV, attending networking sessions, staying in touch with contacts. This is how you increase your likelihood of staying in work.

You should spend at least half-an-hour every day doing something that assists in the process of finding new work. Making contacts. Contributing to relevant discussion boards on LinkedIn. Looking for a few opportunities. Updating your online CV and showreel. Keeping track of companies on Facebook. Looking out for opportunities on Twitter. This time will accumulate over your current contract, meaning you'll be ready to rock when your contract ends, and you'll have a whole raft of warm contacts ready to help you get your new job.

Stay In Touch

I'm often amazed by how many people I've worked with. Camera people I've worked with just once. Make-up artists who've done great work for me on the few occasions I've needed them. Yet when I get a job in, there's only a handful of people who to me are 'front of mind'. This is a phrase used by marketeers to test brand recognition. If I ask you to think of a brand of mayonnaise, odds on you're now visualising the distinctive yellow-labelled, blue-lidded jar of Hellmanns. If I say ketchup, you're likely to say Heinz. This instant recognition factor is being 'top of mind'.

Few people I hire stay in regular contact. That could be saying something about what I'm like to work with! More likely, it's because people don't get around to it, or aren't organised enough to do it. I bet though, that every technician I've hired would like to fit another day's work in their diary every month. If they sent me the occasional email, they might win that work from me. If you're on £200 a day as a make-up artist, and by emailing all your contacts once a fortnight you picked up an extra ten day's work over the year, that's £2,000 or 120 Clinique lipsticks. All for a matter of half-an-hour every two weeks writing an email.

We send a newsletter our to our clients at Napoleon Creative. We don't get a particularly high response rate of people contacting us directly from it. We do see an increase in hits on our website and watches of our videos. What surprises me most is when you're talking to clients and you start telling them about a project and they say 'Oh, yeah, I read about that.' Even if it's just a quick scan down the email, people do take note. Telling people about what work you've done can open up opportunities. If you've only lit talking heads interviews for a production company, but you tell them about the observational documentary you've just shot, they might change the way they look at your work, and the projects they offer you.

The crew who stay top of my mind are Gordon, a DoP who sends out weekly availability emails, Abbie an Editor and Colin an Animator who are linked with me on Facebook and Twitter, and they're constantly sharing really interesting creative stuff. These are the people I think of when I have work to offer.

If you want to increase your sources of work, keep a record of all the people you've worked with. Focus on those who are in a position to give you work, but don't neglect the others who might feed work opportunities to you. Connect with them on LInkedIn, Twitter or whatever social networks you can. Send them out an email newsletter on a regular basis. If you want to be really organised, set up a Mail Chimp account to manage your list and create attractive emails (on brand of course). Be sure to include a clear and 'one click' way for the receiver to unsubscribe.

There is one golden rule to writing these emails: never ask for a job. For me, 'Do you have any vacancies in your editing department?' is a horrible question. Why? Because I have to say 'no.' I know you're asking for work because you don't have any. I've been there, it's a demoralising place to be. I don't want to send you a disappointing note saying 'no, you've no chance here.' I'd rather just let the email slide down my inbox.

Katie is a production and wardrobe designer who writes the perfect 'I'm looking for work' email:

> Hello,
>
> I'm currently working in Wardrobe on a short drama. I have six male principals to dress, and as it's an action script, costumes keep losing buttons and getting ripped, so I'm always at the sewing machine.
>
> We've been in a studio for a month, and now on location in East London until the end of the month. With the end in sight, I'm available to start pre-production on the next one!
>
> I look forward to hearing about any projects you have coming up.
>
> All the best,
> Katie

Funny, insightful about her current job, no hard sell, simply 'I'm going to be available'. Interestingly as well, she doesn't actually ask for a job. She wants to hear about my projects.

She's stayed in touch even though we haven't worked together for over a year, and I know the next time I need a designer, she's the first person I'll call.

Andy, a composer, has already worked for us at Napoleon Creative, so it's easy for him to start a conversation but again he doesn't just ask for work. He shares some of his new work and cheerfully suggests discussing any new projects. This email feels like an invitation to collaborate, not just 'I need a job'.

> Hi Gavin,
>
> I hope all is well and that you are all busy with lots of interesting projects!
>
> Just thought I would drop you a line to let you know some highlights of what I've been up to of late. I've scored for a series on Britain's Top Chefs, an energetic track for a top sports brand and a moodier piece for a fashion house.
>
> Also just completed are more TV documentary series for Sky. As ever, full details and audio clips on my website.
>
> It would be great to discuss any projects that you have coming up that would benefit from some music, or to catch up in general.
>
> Speak soon, all the very best
>
> Cheers
> Andy

And actually, the day he sent this, I had been struggling with music for a piece where the client was being particularly fussy. I'd been looking through library music, but come up with nothing. After he contacted me, I replied and started a conversation about potential music. You never know when serendipity will drop an opportunity into your lap, but you have to be in it to win it. If you're not sending out emails, you're not staying top of mind.

Pick Up The Phone

One day in January, one of the quietest times of the year, two camera people contacted me, both of whom I've worked with before and both I'd happily work with again. One sent a pleasant email asking how things were going and whether there were any opportunities for work. I replied, 'Hey, we've no camera work at present but you're on our list to call when we get the right project in.'

The other called the office. We had a chat about Christmas, being the first time we've spoken since, then discussed my projects, and finally his recent shoots. Of course, future work opportunities came up and he got the same response, we've no camera work at present but you're on our list to call.

Which contact was more effective? Of course, the telephone conversation.

If you're trying to maintain an existing relationship with an employer, use the phone. You might get the 'He's in a meeting' fob off. But if you get to talk to the person, the interaction with them will be more memorable. You'll doubtless be able to fit in some talk about the projects you've done lately. More importantly you can ask about their projects, show some interest in them, and explain why you'd be absolutely perfect to work on them!

In this world of fleeting tweets/bulk emailing/Facebook messaging, if you want to make a real impact go old school and pick up the phone.

Chapter 24

Social Media

Social Media is a treasure map to new contacts, work opportunities and untold riches. Facebook, LinkedIn and Twitter are powerful tools to bring work opportunities your way and are great for 'stalking' companies and individuals by liking, sharing and responding to their posts.

What the map doesn't make clear is that it's drawn over an unmarked minefield... so you must tread carefully. Not a day goes by without a news story generated by a careless or caustic tweet or Facebook posting. Here's my brief overview to using Social Media for finding work.

LinkedIn

You should create a LinkedIn profile as it is a powerful way of connecting with people and showing your prospective employer who you've worked with, and most importantly the contacts you have in common. Whenever we get a new client approach us with a new job, I check LinkedIn to see if I know anyone who knows them, so I can get an inside track on their work modus operandi.

Once you've set up your profile, ask your referees if they will recommend you. You send them a message via the site that directs them to a simple form to complete. This means their recommendation is visible on the site for all to see. There are also countless groups you can join, where you can connect with and learn from film makers from all over the world.

Facebook

Facebook is a handy way of staying in touch with the friends you've made on productions, though inappropriate for making personal introductions to new people to look for work. If you're extending your Facebook friends to include people in higher positions than yours who might offer you work, I'd suggest setting up different levels of privacy to limit what they can see. No one's going to get upset with you having a drunken night out, but your boss just doesn't need to see the details in a photo album!

Facebook is also a good place to 'stalk' production companies to keep up-to-date with what they've been up to. If you see a posting that they've just been commissioned to produce a new series, you can approach them for work perhaps even before they've advertised. And of course, you can 'like' www.facebook.com/cv4tvuk to keep up to date with tips for boosting your TV career!

Twitter

Twitter is a brilliant source of information and job leads. Its open nature means you can have direct access to a surprising number of influencers in the industry, both individuals and organisations, and exchange short messages with them. There's no guarantee that your conversation will be two-way, but it's worth looking into Twitter as a tool for improving your career. It has a very particular etiquette so do some research into how it works before ploughing in.

Vimeo

Constantly evolving and always inspiring, Vimeo is a great site for viewing other people's films and displaying your own. Basic membership is free and enables you to start building your showreel and share your films with the world. It's like being in a room of hundreds of like-minded individuals. Be sure to add Napoleon Creative to your contact list at www.vimeo.com/napoleon!

YouTube

YouTube is an acceptable alternative to Vimeo, especially as broadcasters are increasingly putting their content on specialised YouTube channels. In general, however, YouTube can look very cluttered and has ads. Vimeo is a much cleaner site to watch, and it also allows you to interact with a community of film makers, so personally, I would put more energy into a Vimeo profile over YouTube as you're broadcasting to a more selective audience. You'll probably get more hits on YouTube, but you'll get more targeted views on Vimeo.

Toe in the Water

Whenever you join a social media platform, do so cautiously. Research the platform by Googling the platform plus 'etiquette'. There are thousands of 'Social Media Gurus' blogging advice and top tips to help you find your way. You might go as far as setting up a dummy account on an old email account, so that you can see how it works, test the functionality, see who's interacting on it. That way you can decide whether the platform is right for you before you set up your legitimate presence there.

Privacy

Be aware that your email address can be used to view your presence on any number of personal websites. Remember, people may Google your name to see if they can find information about your career. Your Facebook or Twitter profile might show up in the results. If you have a Facebook account, make sure you have your privacy settings suitably high enough. And everyone enjoys having a silly profile picture, but try to avoid anything that might seem inappropriate.

Over to You

I hope you've found this book as useful as the people who have attended my workshops. They've found a renewed confidence in their skills and how to express them. I trust that by employing the Clearly Creative process, you will too.

Out of all the advice and tips I give in this book, there are six winning principles to keep in your head whenever you're looking for new work:

1. Keep your name, job role and contact number clear
2. Rely on facts not adjectives to show your skills
3. Remain inert to negative reactions
4. Colour your CV so the reader sees you at work
5. Reduce the response time to your applications
6. Stay top of mind

Make this career in this crazy, fascinating, and precarious industry as rewarding as you can.

What's your story?

What's your experience in television? Had a crazy co-worker or an intruiging interview? The world of TV production is full of anecdotes that inspire and pitfalls to be stepped over and we want to hear yours.

Share your stories, ask questions and learn from other professionals at cv4.tv. Find us at your favourite places:

 www.cv4.tv

 www.facebook.com/cv4tvuk

 @cv4tv / #cv4tv

About the Author

Gavin Ricketts is a writer, producer and director with over fifteen years' experience working on both broadcast and corporate documentaries. His first job in the industry was as Production Runner on the feature The Full Monty, when he was studying for an MA in Film Production. Gavin has worked for both the BBC and ITV, including Film 99 with Jonathan Ross for the BBC and National Lottery Draw.

In 2006, Gavin took on the challenge of setting up his own media company, launching Napoleon Creative, which produces high-quality video and animation for clients including Honda, Space NK and Coca-Cola.

Having read thousands of CVs over the years, Gavin set up the cv4.tv website and his Clearly Creative CV workshops to help crew members express their skills and abilities more effectively, to secure interest from potential employers in a competitive market and so increase their earnings and opportunities.

Considered an expert in creative recruitment and an honest and lively communicator, he is regularly invited to present at industry events and film festivals by the likes of ProductionBase, TRC Media and Channel 4.